My Own Financial Blueprint

PRAISE FOR
MY OWN FINANCIAL BLUEPRINT

Ruben Ruiz is one of the most progressive thinking financial planners I have ever met. He not only provides advice but directions to achieve the desired results.

Christopher J. Passero, CPA, MA, Nitro, WV

Finally a must read for those that want a proven path toward financial independence. With practical steps that will take you from point A to Z with a positive mindset and determination to achieve success.

Dr. Juanita Santillan, Chicago IL

This book is the only practical, real-life, no-nonsense reference guide to help Americans to become prosperous and wealthy in the future and for generations to come.

Fraj Lazreg, AIFA ®, CFM, RFC, New York, NY

A must-read, must-own book for anyone who wants save, invest, build net-worth, without having to get a PHD in 'technical savvy' and just have fun while you design your own financial blueprint and then follow the steps.

Alan Lockhart, CEO, Marketing Financial-FMO, LLC, Springfield, MO

In his new book, *"My Own Financial Blueprint"*, Ruben Ruiz shows you exactly what you need to do become wealthy or financially independent and create the retirement of your dreams! Yes, it will take discipline and new habits, but Ruben breaks it down into simple and clear step-his financial blueprint—and therefore takes the mystery out of financial success. The best part? Anyone can become wealthy--high net-worth-you just have to follow the steps. This book is destined to help a lot of people change their beliefs about money and create life prosperity."

Ursula Mentjes, Bestselling author of 'Selling with Intention' and Founder of Sales Coach Now www.salescoachnow.com; Los Angeles, CA

My Own
Financial
Blueprint

The 12 models that build your own money blueprint

Ruben Ruiz

NEW YORK

My Own Financial Blueprint
The 12 models that build your own money blueprint

ISBN 9781614487029 paperback   ISBN 9781614487036 eBook
ISBN 9781614487043 audio
Library of Congress Control Number: 2013939499

Morgan James Publishing   **Cover Design by:**
The Entrepreneurial Publisher   3 Dog Design
5 Penn Plaza, 23rd Floor   www.3dogdesign.net
New York City, New York 10001
(212) 655-5470 office • (516) 908-4496 fax   **Interior Design by:**
www.MorganJamesPublishing.com   3 Dog Design
                                        www.3dogdesign.net

In an effort to support local communities, raise awareness and funds, Morgan James Publishing donates a percentage of all book sales for the life of each book to Habitat for Humanity Peninsula and Greater Williamsburg.

Get involved today, visit
www.MorganJamesBuilds.com.

Habitat
for Humanity®
Peninsula and
Greater Williamsburg
Building Partner

Contents

Introduction

There are twelve chapters in this book or twelve steps and I would tell you that an easy goal would be to read, outline, and study one chapter a month for a year. But something always happens and everyone does things their own way, right! That in itself is not unusual but I will tell you that , the very reason is why the majority of Americans do not know how to create wealth or net worth.

We are taught by our parents, grandparents, relatives, friends, teachers, professors, employers, co-workers, and everybody else everything to do with money. And all or most of that is either completely wrong or many parts are missing. And since we don't know how to build net worth or invest our money, we do what we know and don't find out we are wrong till later in life.

Why is it that only about 6% of all Americans are considered financially independent and have a high net worth? Let's focus on why the other 94% are not wealthy, that is much easier. They have the wrong money mindset and only do what they know how to do, which is usually wrong. Please understand, I am not judging you, and I don't want to tell you what to do with your money.

There are several steps that a person must do to create net worth and wealth, some are technical steps and some are emotional, and some require change of habits. Change is one of the hardest things to do.

Most Americans want to make money fast, or in a short period of time. Because of that, everything that has to do with money is centered on the short term and many other opportunities are missed. There are several steps that you will have to do, and first major step will be to change your money mindset. It's not as easy as you might think.

The Money Mindset will take the longest of all your habits to change, and Chapter One will tell you how. It is also the chapter with the most pages, because there is a lot to cover. Once you understand chapter one, the rest of the book will become easier to take action and implement your financial plan.

Over the years as a financial advisor I have visited with hundreds maybe thousands of people on helping them plan their financial future. I talked with 20 year olds to 60 year olds, before they bought their first home and after they did, when their kids were born and when they turned age 18, when they had their first job and their current job, when they were making $30 thousand to making $80 thousand, when they had a lot of debt to having some debt, and so on, and so on. And do you know that many of those families continued to make the same financial mistakes that they made when they were younger.

Many Americans have different points of view on Social Security, some criticize it, many hate to pay that awful FICA tax, and many want the option to invest that tax in their own investments. What are your thoughts and feelings on Social Security? They may represent your entire Money Mindset. I will tell you that if the US government had given the choice to Americans 40 years ago to invest their own SS payments wherever they wanted to, over 80% would not have one dime today.

If you believe me on that statement, you now know what the money mindset problems are and you can open up your new mindset to start the process of accumulating assets, building net worth, creating wealth, or at very least, reach your goal for financial independence. Yes, you can do this. Just follow the steps, take action, and be disciplined.

You have to ask yourself this question, what have I been doing to build net worth and wealth since high school or college, and what actions have I done right and which ones were wrong?

Read the book in its entirety, outline and outline all chapters, but learn chapter one until you understand the mindset. You will want to read other books on the mindset and other things you need. There is no hurry in building net worth, remember that in ten years you will be ten years older than today, whether you take action on building your financial blueprint or not. Thank you for investing in this book and now go out there and make 10 times, 100 times, 1000 times your return on the investment, it's your call.

Ruben Ruiz.

Acknowledgements

My family and I would like to thank the many wonderful people that are part of the financial services industry. Without their dedication and hard work many Americans today would not have a nice home, an emergency fund, kids with a college degree, a business of their own, a retirement fund, a health-care fund, an investment account, a travel fund account, a charity account, a church account, a wedding account, a grandchild account, a mother-in-law account (some do), real estate fund, a life insurance plan, and many more 'life' accounts for all the dreams and goals of families.

Thanks to my second family at Money Concepts International, with whom I have been associated with for over 25 years. Their staff, employees, and other advisors have supported me and our clients with excellent service and education. Thank you Denis Walsh, the CEO of Money Concepts for your leadership and management of a large financial planning organization that provide us advisors with the business systems and technology tools to run a profitable business.

Thanks to the IARFC & the FPA organizations in Texas and in the United States that provide us with continuing education and financial information that is very important to our business. Thank you Ed Morrow, CEO of the IARFC for your continued dedication of training and education to Advisors, and for your leadership and support of the IARFC.

Thanks to CMG, Marketing Financial, and its staff for their training and education on insurance companies, products and services. Thanks for providing us with speakers & presenters for continuing education and products expertise.

And finally thanks to all the financial advisors, planners, agents, that I have had the privilege to meet and know in my lifetime. They have shared their knowledge and their hearts. Many are true professionals and dear friends.

CHAPTER ONE

My Own Money Mindset

My Own Financial Blueprint what does this mean?

To understand what this phrase actually means, think of a blueprint such as one that might be used for building a house. This blueprint is a set of drawings that shows a builder exactly how a house or other building is to be laid out and constructed. While it might be possible for someone to attempt to build a house without this set of blueprints, it wouldn't be advisable.

Without a blueprint to lay out precisely how a house must be built, the result would probably be a poorly constructed, ramshackle affair that would not be strong enough to withstand the first big wind that came along to blow it down.

So, applying this principle to money, how can the average American go through life without a blueprint to lay out exactly how to build a strong financial house?

With no clear cut, well drafted blueprint to financial success and stability, many people have a house of straw when it comes to money and the first time the Big Bad Wolf comes along---in the shape of a medical crisis, loss of work or any one of the other things that are apt to befall any of us at any given moment---that shaky financial house collapses.

The same people who wouldn't dream of attempting to have a home built without a blueprint will go blithely on, year after year, with no financial plan for handling their money. How do we know this is true? Just look up the statistics on the subject during the past 50 years and you'll see that the proof is in the pudding, so to speak. The same percentage of the population that achieves financial independence is approximately the same as it was half a century ago.

This is remarkable in view of all the new technology we have at our fingertips today. It's also appalling and if you fall into this percentage; more than a little frightening.

If you want to get a set of financial 'blueprints', what do you need to do? Where can you obtain a set of blueprints that will help you build a strong, well constructed financial house with your money....one that won't be blown down with the first hard wind?

What will a set of financial blueprints look like?

Picture it this way: If you have 12 'blueprint' pages and just write out one part of the overall plan for each page, then you will have the full set of blueprints you need for financial well being.

What should be on the first page of this set of financial blueprints? As with plans to build a stable, well constructed house, a financial blueprint should begin with how to build a strong foundation. If the foundation is built on shifting sands, your financial house will not be strong enough and will collapse, taking everything down with it.

If you're wondering what makes up the foundation for your own financial blueprint; it's your mindset. Without the right mindset as the basis of your financial blueprint, you cannot lay a stable foundation that will make a strong base for your money.

What is the mindset of the average American who wants to become financially empowered, wealthy or financially independent? Does the average American even consider the possibility of these things? Most experts say that if you are an ordinary, average, middle-class American; you will never even imagine the possibility of becoming any of the above.

Why not? Quite simply, most of us don't believe it's possible. More importantly, we're taught that financial wealth isn't necessary in order for us to live happy, fulfilled lives. In fact, you'll often hear people say that becoming wealthy actually works against their future happiness, because people who are too focused on building wealth forget about the so-called "important" things in life.

How, then, do average Americans expect to become happy? Most of us just follow the rules for "happy living" we were taught as children:

- Get a high school diploma and maybe college
- Raise a family.
- Get a good paying job.

That's about the size of it. Sound familiar?

Your grandparents and parents believed that making it through school, getting married and having half a dozen kids would result in a great life, or at least a good life. But what does it mean to have a great life? Does it mean having an average income with an average net worth after completing your education and raising a family?

Why be satisfied with being average?

Why shouldn't you have the opportunity to gain wealth—as much wealth as you desire? What's the point of living in the greatest capitalist country in the free world if you can't take advantage of it? Why should you continue living in the days when independently building wealth was virtually impossible, when you live in an era where it happens every single day?!

A strong focus and commitment can take you where you want to go in life, and get you the things you want in life. This is a reality of human nature. Unfortunately, if the scope of your focus does not include becoming wealthy, you're never going to be. Why not? Because you won't be willing to take the necessary steps make wealth come to you. But, even if you have the focus to become wealthy and are rising above the realm of the average Joe or Jane by even entertaining the thought of becoming wealthy, you still might not achieve it.

Focus is nothing without follow through!

Think about your own life. Has your mindset of 'I can't become financially independent, so why bother trying', ever prevented you from exploring or investigating wealth opportunities that could increase your income and expand your net worth? Have you ever discussed financial matters with your parents? What about the idea of becoming financially independent? Did you believe that your family would laugh at the idea and tell you that only certain Americans could pursue that particular goal?

As I said earlier, based on the current median income earned by Americans you can live an average lifestyle in the U.S. You can be "comfortable". But is "comfortable" good enough? Deep down, don't you want more income and more assets for your family? Don't you want something better than just being above the poverty level?

Sure you do!

Just think of all the things you could do if you were wealthy! You could take expensive vacations, not worry about your retirement. You could rest assured that your children's college education is paid for and that they won't have to start new careers burdened with thousands of dollars of debt in student loans. You could buy that new car you've been dreaming about, or contribute hundreds of thousands of dollars a year to charities and non-profit organizations. You could quit your dead-end job and work for yourself. You could do almost anything!

The problem is that we really don't know or comprehend the advantages that wealth can bring us. The grim truth is that most people are never going to become wealthy because the majority of Americans have never been taught how to become millionaires, or wealthy, or even financially independent. Some people believe these terms mean the same thing, while others view them differently.

Which one you are aiming for depends on what you hope to achieve in your future.

In order to become a successful millionaire, who is defined as having a net worth of over $1,000,000, you need to learn how. Since in all probability you don't know and haven't been schooled in how to become wealthy, you will need the right people, tools, advisors or mentors to teach you. You need to bathe your mind with knowledge, on a daily basis if possible but no less than weekly, learning from books, CDs, seminars, workshops, boot camps, teleseminars, the internet, and DVDs.

Complete your formal financial education K12. Just as you started at the bottom rung of grades in your school days, beginning your formal education in the 1st grade where you learned reading, writing and arithmetic, you will need to set your own K12 financial education. It's that simple.

If you're wondering if it will take 12 full years to complete your financial education, the answer is no, it doesn't.

That being said, you do need a program that contains all the financial courses and then implement the study at the times that best suit your schedule. If you don't want to spend some of your free time acquiring this knowledge and education that will teach you how to become wealthy---fine.

Nobody will be standing over you with a ruler, ready to smack your hand if you don't study your financial blueprint to achieving wealth. But, bear in mind that if you choose not to do this, you probably won't be the only person to pay the price of your lack of commitment to learning how to rise above the average and become financially independent, because your family will stay down there in mediocrity with you.

You would probably say that all children should get a high school diploma and go to college, because of what you have learned in your lifetime. College is an important step in expanding your education, as well as gaining valuable knowledge for your career that will help you increase your future income production. College is an invaluable opportunity for young people to interact with their peers. It helps them make the transition from childhood to adulthood and independence. Confidence, social standing, and future business contacts can all be acquired in college, if they have not been before, and are essential components in the life of a future millionaire or just plain 'high net worth'.

But here's the thing: Getting a college degree, or a Masters, or even a Doctorate will not make you financially independent, you still need Financial Education-K12.

So, let's get to the "million-dollar question." How can you become financially independent? Is it possible for you to make $100,000-$250,000 in annual income? The best answer for this is, if you thought that making $45,000 a year was a great salary for you and maybe the max for you in today's dollar, then maybe not. But if you start to think that making $100k is just like making $45k, you will.

However, you'll have to make some changes first.

You're probably already seeing the truth. You're going to have to change your mindset in order to achieve what is dubbed the millionaire goal; which is raising your net worth above a million dollars. You can always shoot for an even bigger goal later—say, a million dollars a year in income—but first things first! You've got to make that first million!

Begin by taking an hour a week to focus on your goal and the steps you will need to take to achieve it. Gradually increase your focus time until the idea of becoming financially independent or drawing up your financial blueprint is as familiar to you as your own name. You might wonder going into this if you are destined to be an average American, making an average income for your family and never climbing out of the pool of just getting by.

Ask yourself some tough questions:

Why have some Americans with the same education and social backgrounds as you become millionaires, while you have continued to make the same, average amount of money?

Do you think you could have a million-dollar net worth? How about a five million-dollar net worth? Ten million? Twenty?

Do you believe that those kinds of goals are unattainable—that only certain Americans are entitled to them?

If you cling to those negative beliefs, even subconsciously, you are setting up a self-fulfilling prophecy—one that will surely keep you from your goal. Let's start the process of believing that you, or any American, can become financially independent.

Begin by altering your ideas of what Americans can do. You might have to live a life that looks very different from the picture that was painted for you when you were a child. This isn't to say that many of the lessons you've learned from your parents, teachers, and peers won't help you. They will. But you must educate yourself on the techniques and experiences you will need to become financially independent.

Start to believe that you have the right to gain wealth for yourself and your family. Most Americans don't know this, but if they can learn the true meaning of 'Belief', or 'Courage', or 'Goal', they can learn whatever else they need to know to attain true wealth. They don't know this because they haven't learned it. They're stuck in the belief that you have to have a college degree, or a great paying job, or a lot of knowledge about Stocks, Real Estate and Investments like some of the 'Money' gurus out there before you can be financially independent.

They're wrong.

Oh sure, eventually you're going to have to know all that. But you don't have to know it right now! You can learn how to become wealthy by setting aside at least one hour a week to learn the system, or the principles, that people have been using to build wealth for years. To be perfectly clear, if you don't build wealth, it is not because of a lack of knowledge. It is because you have fixed habits that you cannot change, because you don't know how to change them. You have been in that 'fixed habit' state for a long time.

But habits can be unlearned and you can learn how to replace those negative beliefs or even subconscious beliefs with new, positive ones that will allow you to believe you can become wealthy.

Always remember: What the mind can conceive and believe, it can achieve.

Let me give you an example. Why do you put toothpaste on a toothbrush? Because it is a habit, right? A good habit! Why do you take a bath every day at around the same time? Do you normally eat three meals a day? Most of the things we do every day are habits, probably most of them are good habits to have, but we all have some bad habits that we would like to change or get rid of, right?

The majority of Americans have 'fixed habits', and fixed money habits. Research has shown that as much as 90% of the population has these fixed habits. So, let's explore habits because understanding habits is one of the secrets, or one of the solutions to your 'money mindset', and eventually your financial blueprint.

How do we develop fixed habits? We learn habits from our parents, grandparents, other relatives, neighbors, school friends, teachers, professors, co-workers, employers, and others. Let's make a factual statement, and you may not believe me, so Google it, and let your mindset believe it. In America only 5-7% of Americans are considered wealthy, or financially independent. That means that 93-95% or more Americans are not wealthy or financially independent. In all probability, you, your parents, your relatives and friends....all included in that larger group of the have-nots.

This may seem depressing, but you have to understand why you are not wealthy or financially independent. Merely reading this book has put you into a minority category of those who manage to rise above the crowd of average citizens. In fact, if you will read this book, and then take action on implementing what is recommended, you will move toward that rarefied top echelon of the 7%. This will be hard to do because your 'fixed mindset' and your fixed habits will work against you to stop you from accomplishing that change.

It's the same fixed habits that stop us from losing weight, exercising, quitting smoking, and so forth.

Developing a money mindset' and creating a 'Financial Blueprint' will take a change of habit. But the change is now a 'growth money habit' or a 'growth financial mindset'. You cannot stop with just breaking a fixed habit in your life. Once you have rid yourself of a bad habit, you should then replace it with a good habit. So, when you have unlearned those self defeating bad habits of believing you can never achieve wealth---develop another habit; the 'growth money habit'.

Few of us remember how we developed habits in the first place, because most of the good habits were ingrained when we were very young. At one point in your school life, you were almost certainly told to take a bath before going to bed, or in earlier life, given a bath before bedtime. Initially, you may not have wanted to take that bath.

But, after a while, the daily habit started to "gel" in your mind. Maybe your teacher and schoolmates made some positive comments to you about your good hygiene and this reinforced your nightly bath ritual. Your parents would say you smelled good. You would begin to interpret being clean and not dirty as a good thing, something to strive for. Before you knew what hit you, you developed a routine of bathing every night. That routine then became a habit.

Wouldn't it be wonderful if we could create a routine, and then a habit, that would make us wealthy or at least financially independent?

Our parents did not know how to do those possible good habits themselves, so how could they teach us the habits that lead to becoming wealthy. 95% of us will have to develop our 'financial habits', our financial blueprints, in our adult lives so that it becomes as ingrained as many other things we do every day.

Once you develop habits that lead you down the road to achieving wealth and financial independence, you have found the 'solution' to dragging yourself up by the bootstraps out of being average.

How are you going to find the time and the energy to develop a new routine and then the new habit, with everything you have to do in your life, in order to survive? You may work eight to twelve hours a day, including the commute, sleep six to eight hours, and take a few hours to nourish your body with food, television time 1-4 hours a day, another two hours to dress and bathe, and how many hours for the kids? Well....that's over 24 hours already and unfortunately, that's the quota for the day.

If this is where you are right now in your life, you aren't alone. The majority of Americans are at the same place today. So how can you change? You will have to take small, baby steps--- one at a time. You will have to develop a routine on what to do every day or week on building net worth and eventually financial independence. For a routine to become a habit, you must plan ahead of time, even up to a year, and then later up to five to ten years in the future. This is hard to do because you have to project your income and expenses in the future and for most of us; anything over a month gives us a headache.

We often don't even like to work out a budget for a month. But, you have to start somewhere, so work on the solution and not the problem.

You will have to set aside one hour a week for you to create your 'Financial Blueprint'. Nothing will happen unless you do something every week, Nothing! You have to be doing something that you have never done before, because you already know that if you do the same things you have done before, you get nothing, right.

It's not the end of the world, as my mother used to say when she gave me a chore that would take a few hours and that I naturally didn't want to do. So, I say to you now: It's not the end of world to become financially independent, is it?

If you can set aside an hour for television, or to play softball, or to party with friends, or to sleep late on weekends, you can find an hour, 'yes I can'. You will have to write down the one hour time slot, on your calendar even your wall calendar, or your planner, or in your computer.

Do you feel better already, we are not through yet, and you will have to write in your one hour time slot for the next 52 weeks. No I am not kidding write it 52 times.

Your mindset is starting to tell you something, your fixed mindset that is, not your 'growth mindset'. Now you can feel the uncomfortable feeling that usually makes you stop whatever you were doing in the past. Not this time, you just have to think about the results of what this new routine will bring for you and your family.

Just do it, as you would do something that was for the benefit or protection of your children. Or get a picture of a bigger home that you would like to live in someday in the future. Or a picture of that one place in the world that you & your wife want to visit.

Okay now that you have set that one hour time slot, what am I suppose to do for an hour a week? Here is a little secret, read a financial or self-help book when you don't have something to do for your blueprint.

During that one hour a week, you will to learn all the steps that are necessary for you to develop your 'financial blueprint', or your financial action plan. Bathe your mind in knowledge, and don't worry about anything else. Your answers will come.

Then, use the power of your life experiences and what you've learned to go out into the world and begin achieving your goals. Instead of a 40 hour work week, make it a 41 hour 'work' week. You work forty hours to make income to pay the bills, and the 'one' hour to create long term wealth.

Is there a secret formula that will help you to become wealthy? The answer to these questions might be obvious to you. You may one day say to yourself, "Duuuhhhh!" Only because when you figure it out, you will know that all the parts are there, and you will know why you had to learn all the parts.

But I'm going to let you in on a little secret. The secret to becoming financially independent or wealthy isn't really a secret at all. The secret is that if you don't believe that the 'Financial Education' formula applies to you, it may as well be written in hieroglyphics…upside down and backward!

Those Americans that have become millionaires did it by focusing on the goal of becoming wealthy, just as they focused on their more "traditional" goals of getting a high school diploma and going to college. If you set your mind to it and go after it with passion and determination you will accomplish your financial goals. That's the so-called "secret" of building wealth. Not too complicated, is it?

To become financially empowered and independent you will have to change aspects of your life-including the people with whom you choose to socialize. Why would you allow friends who make negative comments or list reasons why you can't succeed to derail your millionaire goal? Imagine that you invite your family and closest friends to a party at your home. After dinner you tell them all that you are going to become wealthy. You tell them you intend to be financially independent. What do you imagine will be their first reaction? Will they laugh?

As Americans, we are often programmed to believe that there isn't the slightest chance of becoming financially independent. In our heart of hearts, we may even feel that derisive laughter from friends and family is a normal, appropriate response to our dream. Don't you think that's sad?

If you have made the decision to achieve wealth, why shouldn't your friends support and encourage you? Isn't that what friends are for? I believe there are two reasons why your friends may not live up to this ideal. One is the "misery loves company" principle. If they can't be rich, why should you? The second is that they are afraid. They believe that if you make that leap from the middle class to success you will leave them behind. You know that's not true, and I know that's not true, but they don't know that's not true, and it leads them to say and do things that are going to impede your quest.

Please understand. We are not telling you to forget about your friends. We're simply trying to emphasize the importance of staying focused, because a constant barrage of negativity can delay your progress or even cause you to abandon your dream. Don't let your friends distract you. (And if they're actively trying to do so, are they really, truly your friends at all?)

The reality is that we are all concerned with what our family and friends think. We assume that they constantly wonder about where we are, what we're wearing, and what kind of car we drive, whether or not we should buy a bigger house. Whether this is true or not, the perception drives our behavior.

You've heard of keeping up with the Smiths and the Joneses, right? What do you think the Smiths & Joneses are doing? Well, they are either building their wealth correctly, and that is why they are moving on, or they are building fast and not the right way, and they will crash somewhere down the road.

Have you ever heard statements like, "If you hang out with broke people, you're probably broke too"? You don't want to abandon your lifelong friends and certainly not your family because they don't have the millionaire mindset. Just start adding financially successful people to your roster of friends, while slowly disengaging yourself from negative acquaintances determined to hold you back.

Realize that if you stay middle-income forever, based on United States inflation and tax rates, you will always lead a discontented life-living paycheck to paycheck, not being able to afford the things you really want. There is no free ride to living an independent lifestyle, just lots of hard work.

You will have to become financially empowered mentally before you can achieve your financial goals. This does not mean that you can go out and spend all of your money because in your mind you are already wealthy! True financially independent millionaires are quite frugal.

It will also help if you begin to understand that there is a difference between saving your money and investing it. Millionaires save money on their purchases and they save money for a rainy day, but they use their financial prowess to find, or even create, many investment opportunities that will increase their profits.

Most Americans have no middle- or long-term investment goals, and they are unwilling to take risks to make these investments pay off for them in the end. If you have a die-hard buy cheap mentality created by a lifetime of hearing "traditional wisdom," then you will always think cheap and safe. If you think only cheap and safe you will never have the courage to take advantage of the high profit investment opportunities that are right in front of you.

You may have already passed on some great opportunities because you were afraid that the cost was too high. It may have been too risky, or you may have been afraid that the cost would outweigh the return. You need to change your mindset in order to be successful. If your mindset database has no millionaire files in it, you will never become financially independent!

True millionaires understand that sometimes they have to take a leap of faith. Once you have a clear picture in your mind of yourself as a wealthy person, get up early each morning and put your new ideas into practice. Remember, financial empowerment requires follow through to make it happen!

Now that we've gone over some of the obstacles and even some problems, let me ask you again. Do you believe that you can become financially independent? You have the power. You have always had the power. The power lies in that superb organ we call the brain. It's all in your head! The mind is as precise as a computer, and you can use yours to achieve your dream.

The truth is your mind is the world's most efficient computer, capable of holding billions of bits of information. You may have heard that the average person uses only about 10 percent of the capability of their brain. Although science has proved this to be a myth, the truth of the matter is that most people barely scrape the surface of the enormous potential offered by this amazing organ.

Even if people use 100 percent of their brain, it's very likely that they haven't imported 100 percent of the files they need for making decisions to meet their independence goal. They're using their resources; they're just not using them as efficiently as they could be!

Envision your brain as your personal computer. The things that you are able to do will depend on the files in your computer. You can output only what you input. You can output an Excel spreadsheet only if you input the appropriate data into an Excel program. You can output a letter only if you input the proper characters into a word processing program. If you don't input the proper information, you can't output the proper product!

Of course, you must do more than possess the capability. Every computer has the capability to perform these functions, just as every person has the capability to become wealthy. You must also know how to use the program. Just because you have Excel installed on your computer doesn't mean you will magically receive a detailed spreadsheet of your monthly household expenses. You must learn to identify the data you need and enter it into the program properly.

What happens if your file is incomplete because you have not taken the time to find the correct data?

Your brain's "C drive" has been receiving files since the day you were born. Everything you are able to do in life is stored in a metaphorical file.

Your brain creates output solutions using the data from a combination of many input files.

The right combination of input files can help you create any number of miraculous outputs, even wealth. (Imagine the files Einstein must have installed in his "computer.") One day soon, the right combination of files or folders might help someone find a cure for cancer. The right combination of files will help you become financially independent even sooner.

The right file can mean the difference between owning a $100,000 home or a $250,000 home. It could be a way for you to earn an extra $50,000 worth of income each year. A few strategically placed files can be the difference between your being the person giving a presentation entitled How to become financially independent or the person paying to sit in the audience and listen to that presentation.

A few new files-folders in your brain's computer labeled financial independence can get you out of debt completely. Your computer brain can create a small net worth or a large net worth. So before we move on, let's find out what your computer brain is worth to you today…

What is your time worth? The worth of your time is determined by the worth of your brain, and it is the value of your time that is going to determine whether or not you become financially independent. Throughout this book the emphasis is on the importance of working hard and making sacrifices in your quest to become wealthy. It's true that becoming wealthy requires you to give up some of your free time. What it doesn't (or at least, shouldn't) require is burning the candle at both ends every day of your life until you die. What good is having money if you can't enjoy it?

Millionaires usually become millionaires because they work smarter, not harder. As they accumulate assets their time becomes worth more. The more assets and investments they have working for them, the more they are going to make every minute of every hour of every day. As you get closer to your empowerment goal, the point at which you have achieved your goal of financial independence, you decrease the number of hours you work while increasing the amount you earn per hour. Sounds good, doesn't it?

Let's look at an example. If you are age 45 and make $40,000 a year, and you work 40 hours a week (2,000 hours a year), then you make $20 an hour. If your net worth is $50,000 you can say that everything you have learned in life from birth to the present is worth $50,000. (Divide that by years and you will not like the number).

Is that good or bad? Let's compare with another American, also age 45, with the same education and background. This person works 2000 hours a year and makes $250,000. That's $125 an hour. This person also has a $1,000,000 net worth. Why is there such a huge difference?

You probably know some Americans who make more money than you that have a larger home and a higher net worth. These might be people you've spoken to without ever imagining they could be worth a million dollars. Would you have treated them any differently? Do you want to be in their shoes? Absolutely! Do you believe that you can? These are people just like you who have simply loaded their computer brain with the right type of informational files to obtain the proper output.

Okay, stop reading right now and close your eyes! Repeat these words to yourself: "All I have to do is input the right files into my brain's computer." Say it several times until you believe it. Ignore the strange looks that the dog is giving you. Forget the fact that even your fish have started giving you the eye. This is important!

The idea of inputting new files to change your life is much easier than trying to create a whole new belief system. You already have the things you will need to become financially independent, such as trust, motivation, and self-esteem, and you will be able to access this information whenever you want to increase your future income and create a more substantial net worth. It's all in your computer brain, and what isn't there can be added. All you have to do is input the proper data.

How old you are or how extensive your education was doesn't matter. Your occupation, the value of your home, and the amount of your yearly income don't matter either. Anyone can take the first step down the road to becoming financially independent.

A decade from now you will be ten years older whether you decide to begin inputting your valuable millionaire files or not. You might as well start now and celebrate ten years of prosperity instead of ten years of growing older while standing still.

You have probably heard a several stories about age and too old to start something. Like the mother of four children at age 55 who wanted to go to college but never did. And she said I will be too old when I graduate, and then her friend asked her how old would she be on graduation day, and she said 59. And then her friend asked her how old would she be if she didn't go to college and the 'mother' just gasped, and said the same age 59. She applied for admission the next day. Think, and just change that fixed habit.

You might not realize it, but you have already started the data input process. The information that you have read in this book is already stored in your brain's computer. Are you a little confused? Do you understand the information you have read so far? If the answer's no don't worry about it!

As you progress through the book you will accumulate more facts and tips that will bring the entire process into focus. Wondering what I'm talking about? Here are a few examples of some of the information that will help you input, and a couple of things you're going to need to learn a little more about on your own (which is where the "mind bathing" process during your weekly study sessions comes into play):

My Own Financial Blueprint: Read this book at least five times and outline like you use to do in college or high school. And read other financial & self-help books, whether it's a hardback book, or a Kindle book. Read or review during your one hour a week planning habit.

Real Estate: I'm sure you know what real estate is. You might even have some rudimentary knowledge of the subject. Unless you're a real estate agent, however, you probably have not found the time to input the information you need to acquire real estate and use it to make a profit.

The Internet: Remember when the Internet was new and you didn't understand it at all? Perhaps you needed your seven-year-old to explain it to you. (Embarrassing, isn't it?) Eventually you figured it out though, didn't you? Well, learning the process of becoming financially independent is similar to learning the Internet for the first time. There's a lot of strange and unfamiliar information, and it can be a little intimidating when you first start out. When you have an experienced teacher though, it is easy to learn.

E-mail: When you see the word email, do you think why can't I just use the phone? Well, you probably already know the answer to that. If you don't stay current and up-to-speed, you become obsolete. You have to add new and varied data to your life files in order to create a wealth of knowledge and experience.

See how gaining knowledge and staying up to date on a sometimes dizzying array of changes can help you achieve your goals? The same principles hold true for your quest to become financially independent. Now that you understand how you can input the information and resources you will need to become wealthy, you can begin collecting data and outputting "I am financially independent" into the world.

Do you remember the man from the best-selling book, Acres of Diamonds? He owns thousands of acres of land, and would be considered wealthy by many. His passion isn't his land, however, but the sparkle and shine of the diamonds he covets. Eventually passion turns to obsession, and he sets off on a quest around the globe searching for the precious gems. Eventually he loses everything, sells his land and dies completely penniless. Several years later a diamond mine is found on

his own property. The man was so busy searching for tremendous riches that he never saw the resources that were right under his own feet.

What about the saying that everyone around you seems to say when the conversation is about 'wealth' or money. 'Money is the root of all evil'. Is that statement true? No it's not. It seems everyone that says it forgets a few words that go before it. *The Love of Money is the root of all evil'.* Why do they forget those words, is it because they are broke or poor, or not wealthy?

The average American may think that in order to become wealthy they have to travel far from home. They may believe the town they grew up in is too small to support such big dreams. The truth is, potential wealth exists in your own backyard. Where is your acre of diamonds? Do you already have what you need to attain wealth?

Do you know how to tap your local resources to reach your goals of wealth and financial independence? It's all within reach if you can develop a plan of action to help you find the resources that best meet your needs. Your Mindset today is different that it was when you were 10 years old, you changed it.

You can change your mindset about what it really takes to become financially independent, just input the right info. Just change your routine. Create a growth habit. This is your 'foundation'.

CHAPTER TWO

My Own Planning Process

Now that we have our foundation in place, we will be able to follow our blueprint until it is built, or completed. The rest of the 'financial blueprint' will be items to do or implement, they are not hard, but they will be new to you. You just have to work them one step at a time. Let's go on to the next part of your blueprint, and it is called the 'planning process.'

Most all Americans know what planning means, and how it works, yet they don't plan. We are back to the 'fixed habits' and we don't have a 'growth planning habit'.

Too much in a hurry to get things done, including, 'get rich'. That is why you probably heard of 'get rich schemes', if people think about getting rich quick, then there will always be a 'get rich scheme' available.

And on the other side of the coin, the people that win the lotto, according to the experience & stats, spend all their winnings with-in three years or less. So you can see, Money is not what we might think it is, or how it works, or how to plan for it before we get it, and most important how to plan on spending it after. Let's get to planning.

What is your current 'Planning Process' or a better question might be what is your current "Procrastination Process'? If you don't have a planning process then you have a procrastination process. Always remember 'PP'. The right 'P' will help you achieve your goals, and the other 'P' will not help you reach any goals, financial, or other.

But you are probably doing some things in your life that are on 'automatic', that means you do them every week or every day. Now most all the things you do were probably set by someone else and you had to follow them or else, and they became a habit, whether good or bad. Hopefully most are good.

In chapter one we talked about the fixed & growth habits, and we will discuss a few similarities on habits in the planning chapter. Now you know how important 'changing habits' are, and also how they affect two important parts of your blueprint. Not to mention that the more you read on the same subject, the faster the retention, the quicker to reach your financial goals.

Let's look at some examples: When you went to school from 8 am to 4 pm every day, dictated by your parents & law, you did this every day till you graduated. You were on automatic. When you started your work or job career, you worked from 8-5 pm (normal), which was dictated by your boss & money, right?

How about some personal habits that are on automatic now; You eat three times a day, you take a bath at least once a day, you go to sleep every night. Now these are good habits and you are doing them without realizing, that they are 'on automatic'. So from a 'Planning' process someone helped to plan these habits for you, Parents, Teachers, and Employers. So all you have to do is implement a 'Planning Process' on achieving wealth or financial independence.

That means you have to set up your system to be on 'automatic'. Achieving any financial goal or any other goal in your life, means it has to be on automatic, either every day or every week. As we said earlier if you can set aside one hour a week, you can reach your financial goals. Believe it or not most Americans don't set one hour a year to 'Plan' their financial future. That means that the majority of Americans are doing the other 'P', which is, 'Procrastination'.

Okay so let's begin, with our 'one hour' a week financial planning session. First let's find a place that we can plan every week that is quiet and without any interruptions. That could be your home, apartment, worksite private area, library, coffee house, and so forth.

Next select the one hour during the week that is best for your 'Mindset'. Is it at 6 am on a workday and you still have plenty of time to get to work on time? Or 6 pm after work, or Saturday morning at 10 am, or Sunday afternoon at 5 pm. Put in your computer calendar/ appointment planner for the next 52 weeks, yes for the next 52 weeks. You have to make an appointment, and commit every week.

There is nothing hard about doing your 52 week calendar; you and the majority of Americans have not done it before, or your best friend or relatives, or teachers, or co-workers. Now you know why only a small percentage of Americans have wealth.

Pick the time and day of the week that you feel you can commit to every week. This does not mean that you cannot change the day & time, and you can because the most important goal is to do every week. But the best way to change the day & time is to change it in advance of that time slot.

You don't want to change on the day & time of your session, because it is very easy to get into the other 'P' word, procrastination, and you do something else because you are thinking that you can always move it. That is what procrastination really is, moving things you need to do to another time. You know what I mean, 'I will get around to it', or 'tomorrow', any excuse will do.

Okay now what is the first item to do at your first planning meeting? Set your 'goals', write them out in your computer or in a notebook. You should set 'short-term' goals, 1-3 years, 'medium-term' goals, 4-10 years, and 'long-term' goals, more than 10 years. Now before we start on our goals we must address the question 'what if I don't write down my goals, or I don't like to set goals.

Goals are hard to set because it deals with forecasting your future, and plus we did not study 'how to do goal's' in school, so I hate goals, and my brain starts hurting when I am trying to set goals. That's why Americans who don't set goals are not wealthy or financially free. You have to view 'planning' and goals just like you would view a 'Stock' to buy or a piece of 'Real Estate', you know that you have to invest in either to make money.

All wealth goals come with risks. That includes the goal of creating a million dollar net worth or becoming wealthy. But here is the bigger truth: there are risks for everything we do in life. The key lies in learning how to counteract those risks. We protect our families by providing shelter and teaching them our values.

We get our children immunized so they'll be less likely to get sick. We take out insurance policies to protect ourselves and those we love in the event of a catastrophe.

Yes, there are risks all around us, but we combat those risks by educating ourselves and by taking action. There is no difference regarding the quest to become a millionaire through multiple investment plans. There are inflation risks, debt risks, tax risks, as well as diversification and emotional risks that have an effect on wealth investing. And 'Planning' and goal setting is another risk that probably has the greatest impact on your financial planning goals.

You can't reach a net worth goal or pay off any debt without putting some work or effort into the goal. There are no short cuts. You won't develop wealth without investing or taking some other action. Planning, or the "P" word, is the essence of success. It is knowledge that creates the resources that give you the power to take action. It is the power to find out what inflation, debt, taxes, diversification, and emotion can do for your personal success goals.

You must create your financial goals, and you must use every resource and professional available to help you succeed. Planning will require you to write out your goals. Then they have to read those goals at least weekly, if not daily, until they become very clear. When your goals are clear and you implement steps to reach them, action and results follow.

Don't be afraid of success. But do understand that you will have to make changes in your life. As you plan and set goals, you will realize that you may have to miss some of your normal weekly activities: Sunday football games, PTA meetings, some kids' activities, lawn work, or golf game. While these activities are certainly important, if you allow such activities to fill up all your free time every week, you will never accomplish your bigger goals for you and your family.

You need to get on the positive goal track. Once you start your, planning and meeting goals, your successes will help you concentrate all your power, energy, and talent to reach your 'financial' destination. You will naturally receive the enthusiasm you need to get to the next stage. Your goals will help you develop confidence in yourself, and build your self-esteem.

Writing down your goals will help you make the right decisions for your wealth building. Your goal plan will produce opportunities for you that you never would have seen if you didn't have a plan. Finally, your plan will give you the impetus to overcome any obstacles that get in front of your goals.

Okay now you are at your first 'P' meeting with yourself, you have to ask yourself, 'what are my financial goals'. You can start out with what is your current income & expenses, and how can you 'save' or invest' more money from your paycheck. You may just write down the goal, to save 3% more of my paycheck. That's good for your first 'short-term goal. Then you might write down a 'medium-term goal', like in five years, we will need $ 10,000 for a down payment for a bigger home.

For a 'long-term goal', you could write, a 'million dollar' net worth in 20 years. Now a 'million dollar' net worth in 20 years will have to be a higher number because of inflation & taxes, let's just say it's two million. Don't' get worried, everything else will go up too, including your income. Now this may look like a hard goal to reach but let's break it up over the next 20 years.

There will be details of how to build a million dollar net worth ($2 million) in twenty years in the Net Worth chapter.

Almost all Americans do not know how to build wealth. They could double or even triple their net worth by planning more and learning all areas of building wealth. Let me tell you a story about how planning can work for you.

Jack and Leslie were given the opportunity to own a business in the communication industry. Besides the minimum capital that Jack & Leslie would need, the owners said they would also have to pass a test designed to make sure they had the "right stuff "to run a successful business. They were given a list of ten items that they had to find in different locations around the city. Each item came with a sophisticated clue that told Jack & Leslie where the items could be found. They followed each clue meticulously until they located each item. They planned after they found each item, until they reached number ten, or until they became successful with their plan.

When you read this story, can you see how planning relates to success? A plan serves as a detailed report that gets you to the next step in your goal. More planning gets you to the next action item required for success. You take it one step at a time. Most Americans never get to the first clue because they don't know where to look for the resources, or they don't want to take the time to sit down and put their new resources into action. Don't neglect the power of planning. It truly is a valuable key to reaching your financial goals.

Here are the "Planning' steps;

1. *Set up your one-hour planning session time & day.*
2. *Set up your session in a place with no distractions.*
3. *Keep the appointment with yourself every week.*
4. *Use computer folders or a manual binder with tabs.*
5. *Create a checklist for everything you are planning.*
6. *Have a calendar that includes weekly, annual, 5 years.*
7. *Have outline of your goals & action plans.*
8. *Have your short, medium, & long-term goal sheets.*
9. *You will need your net worth worksheets for all years.*
10. *You will need your cash flow worksheets for all years.*

Now you are ready to initiate your action plan by learning how to create new assets, increase your net worth, choose appropriate investments, protect your assets, diversify your assets, and leverage and manage your time. Good luck. Here's where the journey really begins!

You may be thinking that you can't possibly take time out of your hectic schedule to set up a calendar. If you're not thinking that, you will be in a minute when you see how detailed you need to be to make it! But if you continue doing what you have been doing for the past five years—living without a financial planning calendar, where will it get you? Basically, it will get you where you are right now. Slowly but surely you have to make a "wealth change," and your calendar is the beginning.

Before you actually set up your calendar, take time to review what goes on in your normal twenty-four-hour day.

Write out the times or number of hours that you spend for the following:

- Sleeping and eating habits
- Your daily commute
- Work hours
- Your family obligations
- Social activities

Do one set for work days and one set for weekends.

All of the above time slots can now be filled in around your weekly one-hour planning sessions, until you are done. While writing out what you will do in the future is one of the most difficult tasks in the wealth-building process, there is no other way. Of course, you will have unavoidable changes in your schedule because of work events, sick children, and other personal matters, but as long as you get your "one hour" in sometime during the week, you'll stay on track.

By the time you add the time slots for your entire weekly schedule for all fifty-two weeks, you will have a full year of work and play ahead of you. As each week approaches and your schedule becomes a "firm up," schedule you can fill in the time for your vacations, special weekend plans, and holiday events. This will, no doubt, require some coordination with your spouse.

You didn't know you were that busy, did you? By having your calendar in front of you at your weekly one-hour meetings, you can start to make important changes in your schedule to fit your financial success goals. There will probably be some social or holiday events that you will have to miss in order to accomplish your wealth goals. Don't forget to add important contacts and other resource information on your calendar.

For instance, you will want to add your financial advisory team members, which will be covered later on in the book. Take your calendar with you wherever you go.

This should help you to see the benefits of getting more structured. Before long, you will see the fruits of your labor really start to pay off.

CHAPTER THREE

My Own Income System

The ultimate financial goal is to build a net worth, and the foundation & funding of that goal will come through your income system, whether you have a structured one or an unstructured one. Most Americans have an unstructured system and will have a net worth hopefully, but those with a structured system will have more, a lot more.

Our structured system is about setting percentage goals (%) on all the income we receive before we write checks or transfer to different outflows or expenses. By setting up a percentage (%) of our income we don't over spend on the other accounts. This is what Businesses do (or try to do) on their income & expenses. This is one of the first things that their CPA or bookkeeper will tell the business owner. If they don't do it, they have a good chance of 'going out of business.' So that's what can happen to your personal family 'income' business, you can go out of business, or not achieve the net worth goal that you want.

Let's break down what we need to have for our own Income System. First we need to list all our income. Income includes salaries, commissions, fees, bonuses, dividends, capital gains, net rental income, and interest. For your salary or paycheck, which is what the majority of Americans earn, it's your gross pay check before any deductions or withdrawals.

Expenses/Outflows is everything that is spent or saved. This includes include mortgage payments or rent, utilities, taxes, food, entertainment, educational expenses, child care, medical expenses, insurance, vacations, loan payments, credit card payments, savings, retirement, church/ charities, and special events, and so on.

Your financial goal is to make the income/revenue side equals the outflow/expense side of your chart. Sounds pretty simple, right? Your income minus your expenses equals your personal net profit or savings/ investment amount. The more you increase your savings, the more money you will have to invest. The more you invest the more assets you create. The more assets you create, the more you're net worth increases and the closer you are to your Financial Independence or Wealth Goal.

To create your own Income System, you will need a monthly worksheet, one for each of the twelve months in a year. You can do manually and store in a binder or on your computer. Any spreadsheet can work or make your own. This is different than a monthly budget, but it is similar.

Let's draw out a monthly worksheet;

List all your income sources by name, one per row.

This includes your salary, spouse's salary, interest, net rental income, dividends, commissions, bonuses and capital gains. If you are close to retirement or in retirement, then your income sources that you will add include; Pension check, Social Security check, retirement plan check, or other checks, just name them and write them down.

For most of you that are starting to build your net worth system, you will probably have one or two salaries to input. This is the easy part, just look at your paycheck. Now this is monthly, so if you are getting paid weekly or bi-weekly, you should total for the year and divide by 12 for monthly.

Now you will list your outflow which includes expenses and savings, whether it's a short term or long-term account, this is where the system comes in. We want to set up percentages (%) for each category of outflow/expenses, and then the percentage of each item. But first you have to list all the expenses or outflows, and then you can group by category. While you can name your categories any name you want, here is what we will be using in the book. (You can give each a code name and make a game out of it to do monthly).

There are seven (7) categories of outflow and you can change the title of each, which you and/or your spouse may prefer.

1. *Capital Accounts*
2. *Eventful Accounts*
3. *Knowledge Accounts*
4. *Debt Accounts*
5. *Give Accounts*
6. *Play Account*
7. *Means Accounts*

Let's indentify what each account means and we will also include a percentage goal for each account. You will have to make the percentage goals fit your cash flow in the beginning to make your Income System work and undo your old system.

Capital Accounts-10%: These are long-term accounts to put money away and hopefully never touch the principle and in your work years not the earnings either, if possible. This is for your future and these accounts will determine whether people call you an old man, or a retired gentleman. Some of the accounts that you will have in this category include; IRA's, 401k, Mutual Funds, Stocks, Bonds, Pensions, Life Insurance Savings, Annuities, Real Estate.

Eventful Accounts-10%: These accounts can be short-term, middle-term, and even long-term accounts. If you don't have these accounts, you will still need to have the money for whatever event comes up and you do not have any savings. These events are usually what puts families behind or increases their debt. Eventful types are the special events that happen in your life and will cost a good chunk of money. Normally if the expense was an optional type, you wouldn't do it.

For example; A down Payment for your home; College Money for your kids; A Sweet Sixteen Birthday Party for your daughter; A wedding event; Addition to your present home. There are many more.

Knowledge Account-10%: This account is to have monies available for continued learning & financial education to teach you & your spouse how to build wealth and net worth. This would include; Books, Audio CD's, DVD's, Workshops, Seminars, Coaching programs, Schools, Computer Hardware & Software, Boot Camps, and so forth. Knowledge will help you to get to your goals quicker, which means you are making more earnings on your net worth and it increases faster. It will also pay for itself plus more.

Debt Accounts-10%: The Debt account is used to pay off your debts quicker and of course save interest paid out to another party, instead of you. This account is used to pay off the principal balance quicker. When we discuss your Means Account, you will see that your minimum payments for Debt are in this category, but your accelerated payments over the minimum will come from here. One day in the future you will have paid all your Debt Accounts, and you can now shift the 10% allocated here to your Capital Account or any of your Accounts.

Give Account-5%: The Give account is the account you use for your church, charities, and non-profit organizations. Eventually you can increase this account to whatever percentage is perfect for you and your family. You probably think that it is strange to set aside money to give, when you need every dime to live on or make payments, right? That is true and you are the only that can decide how to allocate your outflow or payments.

The long term effect of Giving will help make you wealthier. Believe or not if you remember that we said in the first chapter, it's your Money Mindset that will help you achieve your goals. A person or family that gives money all the time means that in their Mindset, they can always make more money than whatever they give. You have probably heard the saying, 'the more you give the more you get back'. The other side of giving is that it makes you feel warm to help or support an organization or people.

Play Accounts-5%: This is the account you use to have fun, and it is also the category where many Americans spend too much and then get into financial trouble. Can this account increase, of course it can, and it's how you handle the other accounts. But you can use this account for weekly 'Play' activities, or you can read a good book, or attend some free events in your community, and save the 5% and then use it up once a month for a bigger 'play' entertainment event. For example, you and your spouse could go out of town for the weekend at some place you have not been to.

Means Accounts-40%: This is the account that you pay for everything else for your family, or the costs that each family needs to live in a comfortable lifestyle. The Means account percentage that is allotted for each family monthly Income System will be different. For some they may need 50-60% for their Means Account, which all the other accounts will have to be adjusted too. You may have to put money in the Capital Account or Eventful Account that is less than the model presented here for a while.

The Means account is really 'Living within your Means' and not spend money you don't have, or to spend for items that are really not needed for the family. You have to cut somewhere and for certain items. The Means Account include; Mortgage Payment or Rent, Groceries,

Utilities, Transportation, Insurance, Taxes, Personal Care, Credit Card-Loan Payments, Miscellaneous.

You will use your cash flow worksheets (CFW) to create your income/expense chart for the current year. You will need twelve (12) CFW's for one year and you will probably make many adjustments on both your CFW and your wealth chart. That is good. The more adjustments you make, the more you are focusing on your financial goal.

You will start to account for every penny you spend because you know every dollar spent cannot become an asset.

Use your checkbook and credit card statements to keep track, and make a "cash jar journal" to account for each bit of cash you spend. Whatever you spend money on with cash, you either get a receipt or make a receipt on what you spent, and then put into a jar.

At the end of month you simply post each receipt to a journal, add your checks & credit cards purchases, and you will be very close to 100% of your spending. Your cash jar journal will show you what's happening on the expense side of things. Do this monthly or even weekly, depending on the timeline of your goals and when you pay your bills.

Since the days before Christ, numbers have been constant. People lie, but numbers never do. If you don't keep accurate records of where your money goes, how will you know where you stand financially? Run your household like a business, and one day, you will have a very profitable household. When that day comes, you will be glad of the small sacrifices you made along the way.

Americans are taught that in order to be successful in the United States, one must get an education. If you finish high school and then go on to complete a college education, you can expect to find a good job, which really means that you can expect a nice monthly paycheck. The "real world" begins when you become a W-2 or 1099 (for commission work) employee. You are paid based on the hours you work. The majority of Americans enter the workforce as W-2 hourly employees.

Your employer is mandated by the IRS to deduct federal income taxes and social security contributions from each paycheck. The IRS knows how difficult it is to send a lump sum tax payment at tax filing time, and they have enough taxpayers who are paying on the finance plan. While you may not like to pay taxes through your paycheck (or even pay taxes period), this is the easiest way to get the job done.

In order to become wealthy, you must learn to save or invest your own money the way you pay your taxes to the government. "Deduct "it from your check before you spend it. Learn how to save and take time to research possible investment opportunities.

If you don't trust yourself to put money aside each pay period, then have your employer deduct the funds and put them aside for you through your 401(k) or salary allotment to your bank or credit union savings account. Many people are afraid of the idea of a lower take-home net check, but it won't take long at all to adjust to a new, slightly more modest lifestyle.

The secret to becoming wealthy is not really a secret at all. We create the mystery because we are afraid to implement the necessary change in our financial lives. The "secret" is to create assets. You can do this through savings accounts, investment accounts, retirement accounts, and real estate accounts. You can determine your net worth by taking your total assets and subtracting your liabilities.

The 'secret' is to transfer a percentage of your monthly income check into an asset.

There are quite a few secrets that have been mentioned in the book, but the reason on saying it's a secret is because there are no secrets, but either we don't what they are, or if we do, we take them for granted because we have heard about them so much, we don't really believe the 'secrets' are really principles that have lasted thousands of years. That means they work.

How do we make something so simple seem so difficult? Americans have one of the most educated populations in the world, and yet we have one of the lowest savings rate: the average American saves about 4 percent from his or her annual income. Why is this? Americans have been programmed via the media to spend first and save later.

We are born procrastinators when it comes to saving money. In fact, many people are so well programmed that they spend money they don't even have. Charging goods and services on a credit card creates an even more threatening demon, debt, one of the worst enemies you can face.

The real secret of wealth, the one every self-made millionaire eventually learns, is that you must save a certain percentage of your income every month first. Then, and only then, you can spend the net. A reasonable goal is to start at 10 percent of your paycheck, and live on the remaining 90 percent, an amount that in your new empowerment mindset becomes 100 percent. You may have to start with a goal of less than 10 percent and then increase the amount every month, or every quarter, or every year.

There are a number of ways to save automatically each month. You can set up automatic payroll deduction that will deposit money into retirement or savings plans. You can also set your checking account on automatic draft.

It doesn't matter which method you choose. Your goal should be to set up some kind of system that will keep you from spending money on pricey restaurant meals, gadgets, new cars every two years, or whatever "toy" strikes your fancy. As you monitor your monthly paycheck, cut wasteful expenses and pay off your debt, you will find it easy to reach your monthly savings investment goals.

For example, you can set up a plan to start saving 2 percent of your paycheck, and increase it by 2 percent every quarter or every six months. When do you stop saving this way? When you can no longer live a lifestyle that's acceptable to you or you run out of money for your bills. Do you think this will be difficult to do? Of course it will, at first.

Becoming wealthy does take some hard work. If it were easy, everyone would be a millionaire! Each month that you increase your savings investment accounts, you increase your assets column (the left side of your balance sheet).

While it may be difficult in the beginning, you have to pass this challenge. You will probably have to adjust your lifestyle and substitute inexpensive life activities. As your assets and income increase, you can adjust again.

As a W-2 income employee, you will save a percentage of income. If you are a business owner, you take your gross income minus business expenses, and save a portion of income too. That is the secret. Your income stream can create all the assets you want: savings accounts, investment plans, retirement plans, stocks, mutual funds, and real estate.

Let's look at an example:

Robert and Rita work as W-2 employees. Robert is a welder and Rita works for the state. Their gross paycheck is $5,000 a month, and their take home is $3,750. They are thirty-five years old and they begin saving 10 percent a month ($375), correct? No, that is what many people might think. But it is 7.5% of their gross income that is what you work on.

They also set a goal to increase their savings by 2 percent every year until age fifty. When they reach fifty, they will have accumulated $100,000, based on an average return of 5 percent. If they had earned a 12 percent rate of return, that amount would have been $360,000.

Here's an interesting truth: once you start living a more modest lifestyle, you will likely find that you need fewer and fewer material 'things' in order to be happy. You will learn how to substitute free or inexpensive activities for your compulsive spending—hiking with your family, reading books checked out from the library, renting DVDs instead of going to the movies, etc. You will learn that fulfillment doesn't have to come with a price tag—and that realization alone makes the Empowerment Goals worth pursuing.

From your Income System you will start to create assets, like a savings account, 401k or IRA account, a Mutual Fund Account, and many more accounts. When you add these assets together they equal your total assets. This is listed on the left side of your balance sheet.

Then on the right side you would list your liabilities, and as you implement the Income System, you are reducing your liabilities side. When you subtract the total liabilities from your total assets, you get your own 'net worth'. Your 'net worth' is a picture of your value or worth, and will cover this in the next chapter.

CHAPTER FOUR

My Own Net Worth

Net Worth is the big picture of your value, of your assets. It lists all your assets & liabilities. Net Worth equals your assets minus your liabilities. Let me give you two statistics that can help you realize how important net worth is. Then, when you look at your net worth and make comparisons, you will see that you are in the middle, or just average.

More than 30% of Americans have a negative net worth, that means more liabilities (or debt) than assets (if any). Unless they find a way to get out of a negative net worth they will always depend on the government for support or help.

About 5% of Americans have a net worth greater than $500k, and only about 2% have more than a $1 million dollar net worth. Since only a small minority of people in the US has a high net worth, that means there is a lot of opportunity for you to achieve a high net worth goal. A million dollar net worth goal is a great goal to start with, whether it takes you ten years or twenty years or more.

Think of it this way: The years will go by whether you are amassing wealth....or not.

The balance sheet is the accounting form that shows your net worth. On the 'left' side of the balance sheet is where your assets will be, and the on the 'right' side is your liabilities. Your net worth is listed on the bottom left side. When you add together both sides, the amount will be the same. Assets – Liabilities = Net worth. Or, Assets equal Liabilities + Net Worth.

There are numerous assets that you can create or build over time. Here are some examples:

- Checking account
- Cash
- Savings Accounts
- Money Markets
- Certificates of Deposit or CDs
- Treasury Bills
- Treasury Notes
- Treasury Bonds
- Municipal Bonds
- Government Bonds
- Corporate Bonds
- Stocks
- Mutual Funds
- ETFs or Exchange Traded Funds
- Annuities
- Life Insurance Cash Value
- Silver
- Gold
- Diamonds or other jewels
- IRA

- ROTH
- 401k
- 403b
- 457
- Pensions
- Real Estate
- Business Equity

On the Liabilities side you could have, or will have:

- Mortgages
- Auto Loans
- Credit Card balances
- Bank or Credit Union Loans
- Margin Loans
- Real Estate Loans
- Commercial or Business Loans
- Taxes Payable
- Personal loans from friends or relatives.

Increasing your asset side---or decreasing your liability side---increases your net worth. The return on your assets increases net worth.

In order to build your blueprint for the net worth section, you have to do a balance sheet today and see where you are.

This is Net Worth sheet Number One.

If you remember from the previous chapters, we used the long-term goal of a million dollar net worth, which in 20 years with inflation would be about $2 million net worth.

You would not create a balance sheet showing a net worth of $2 million, and you would number this sheet as number 20. You would also put in the date of the balance sheet as 20 years from the date of your year one net worth statement.

So now you have Year One net worth, which you probably don't like very much. Next, you have Year Twenty, which looks great. Now all you have to do is match up the 18 years in between and voila!---you will reach your goal.

Does that mean you have to populate the 18 balance sheet statements between number one and number 20?

Yes!

You will produce 18 financial net worth statements or balance sheets. Now you have twenty net worth sheets, numbered from 1 to 20, and by years, depending on the date you start this.

Yes, twenty net worth statements or balance sheets! You may be thinking that this sounds pretty dumb. But, remember: it's your fixed habits versus the growth money habits that you don't have. Also, do you know what high net worth Americans do to achieve their net worth? When you look at it that way, it's not dumb anymore.

On the 20th year, you will write at the bottom of the page----Net worth = $2,000,000. Above that number you will write out all the assets that you expect to own, as well as the liabilities you hope to *not* have or, at the very least, have with a low balance.

Okay, you have done the hard part!

Now from year 20 to year one, you just populate the numbers from the 20 year number to the 19th year statement and fill in the numbers & assets with a number below the 20th year number of 2 million net worth. You lather, rinse and repeat, doing this all the way to your present year position. Put them in a notebook or a computer folder and you are on your way to reaching your long term goal of $2 million net worth.

What happens when you get to a year and it is below the goal amount that you should have by that time?

You adjust. This is what financial planning is all about. Goals are made to be adjusted. That's the nature of building net worth and other financial goals. You make adjustments as necessary.

Every year you will do the same exercise you did a year earlier. The difference is that every time, you will do one less balance sheet. Each year you will do this exercise to keep you on track and take action. What will happen is this: it will help you get to your goal faster, or it will take you longer than the 20 years to attain your goal. But, who cares as long as you hit your goal, right? Better late than never!

Now let's get to work and look at ways to increase your net worth every year along with how to do that based on your risk tolerance.

All investments have different levels of risk.

Let me give you a classic example to compare: an average CD return is 3%, and the average Growth Stock Fund is 11%. If that was all you needed to know, you would probably take the Growth Stock Fund. But, if we look at risk tolerance, based on the historical past , we find that a CDs average is a low of 1% and a high of 6%. On the Growth Fund it shows a high of 28%, and a low of minus -22%. That sheds a different light on which investment you would select doesn't it?

We will talk more about the 'Market' in chapter 8. For now, let's focus on average returns, or estimated returns, based on past history. Plus we'll look at returns after taxes. We could say that if you only put money in very conservative financial instruments it would be a matter of time and you would hit your million dollar goal.

This is true. You will either save or invest your entire salary, or invest for 100 years to reach your goal. Now you understand why each investment has its return model. You must understand how diversification works to get you that average return you need. Or, if you want to not diversify and select investments that average higher returns, you will have higher returns than the diversification model.

It boils down to how you can handle a drop in the market or a negative return year, emotionally.

Let's start with compounding of your returns and see how that compares with simple interest.

Albert Einstein called the compounding of money the "eighth wonder of the world." I'm referring specifically to the process of compounding your earnings on investments and multiplying your wealth over time.

Remember, either your money compounds over time as you age, or you just get older without any compound return. Since you are going to age anyway, why not take advantage of those years and make a good compound return on earnings at the same time? Doesn't that make good financial sense?

Let's look at an example: If you deposited $1 in a bank in the year 1 A.D. and the bank paid simple interest of .005 (1/20th of 1 percent), your $1 would grow to $21 in the year 2000. But if your dollar compounded at .005 for 2000 years, you (or one of your heirs) would have a balance of $1,182,049,000. That's over one billion dollars, just by compounding.

Wow! Big difference huh?

Now let's do a more current & real example: A couple puts away $100 a month in an investment account that is projected to pay 4% for the next thirty years. In thirty years the couple would have $69,636.

At $200 a month, this amount would double to $139,272. After educating themselves on investments and returns, the couple decides to change their investment to an account (or portfolio) that has averaged 10% over the last twenty years (Called Historical Return). At $100 a month with a 10% projected return for thirty years, the amount equals $227,933.

Double the figure to $200 a month and you get $455,866. That's a difference of more than $300,000 over the same thirty-year period on the 4% projection.

This example was built on investing or saving the same amount of money each month. What will happen if you implement a plan to increase that amount by 10% every year? $220 a month the following year and so on? You will have different amounts to total.

If you invested $10,000 in an investment account with a ten year return of 12% and you were able to make the same return for the whole ten years, your investment would be worth $31,058. How does this work in real life to accomplish your financial planning goals?

Let's take another couple who sold their first home and decided to invest the $25,000 profit. They are purchasing their second home and maximizing their mortgage financing. They invested the $25,000 in U.S. Treasury Bills with an average historical return of 4% over twenty years. Twenty years at the 4% amount will yield $54,778. What would have happened if this couple had put their $25,000 profit into a diversified portfolio with a historical return of 10% for twenty years? They would have a grand total of $168,188. Simple, is it not?

It is important to understand that just because an investment has ten, twenty, or thirty-year historical returns, it does not mean that you will have the same returns in the future. But using an historical return is a good starting place to project your future net worth and future values. Now we can make this eighth wonder of the world a little easier to understand.

All you need to know is your current age, and how to divide your projected rate of return by seventy-two. This "Rule of Seventy-two" will tell you how many years it will take to double your money. All you need is a piece of paper and a pencil and you can follow the next three examples.

Let's use age 40, a $10,000 investment, and 4%, 8%, and 12% as projected rates of return. We now divide each of the three rates of return by seventy-two.

72/4% = 18 years   72/8% = 9 years   72/12% = 6 years

-RULE OF 72-

	4%	
Age 40		$10,000
Age 58		$20,000
Age 76		$40,000

	8%	
Age 40		$10,000
Age 49		$20,000
Age 58		$40,000
Age 67		$80,000
Age 76		$160,000

	12%	
Age 40		$10,000
Age 46		$20,000

Age 52	$40,000
Age 58	$80,000
Age64	$160,000
Age 70	$320,000
Age 76	$640,000

The biggest mistake that many people make every day is only focusing on the $10,000 today, without being able to envision the future value. They don't know how 'planning' works and they don't understand 'compound interest'. Two small concepts that produce a difference of $600,000 and each started with the same $10,000 investment one time. How about if you invested another $10,000 several times, instead of only once?

Now you can calculate the projected net worth of all your investments. Compound earnings really are magical. When you double your return from 4% to 8% your compound net worth increases four times. When the value goes from 8% to 12%, the values multiply by four again.

Now you know why compound interest is called the eighth wonder of the world. And you're probably starting to see how it can help you to become wealthy---either a millionaire or financially independent.

What's not included in the samples using compound return, are two major items, what type of investments can make 12%, and how those investments are taxed. Most of the investments types or accounts will be covered in the 'Stock Market' section, or 'the Market' for short. Because the actual 'Market' has more than just stocks, as you will see later.

The second major item that is not included in the sample returns is how your investment is taxed.

Do you pay taxes this year, or in the year of the gains or interest paid, or is it tax deferred or postponed till the future? Is it tax-free or subject to capital gains? How your investments are taxed also requires its own chapter.

CHAPTER FIVE

My Own Capital Management

What is Capital Management?

You can interpret capital management however you want to, but there are at least three parts to the system. You should want to utilize all three. The three parts are:

- Debt management
- Cash flow management
- Savings management

Debt management is the process of paying debts in the shortest period of time that you can manage. Savings management is the process of saving as much as possible every month. Cash flow management is the process of managing your income, living expenses, debt, and savings. What would you do, given that you have two choices, to pay off debt? Would you focus on paying debt first before you start a savings program, or would you do both at the same time? With the first method, you will pay off your debts faster. Once your debts are all paid, you can start saving the payments that were used for those debts.

This is exciting!

It may not always be as easy as it might sound. You might be sailing along, putting a big dent in the balance of your debts every month, and then get blindsided by an emergency that crops up, and need the money for that crisis rather than to pay down your debts.

If this occurs, all you can do is adjust. Pay what you must to meet the financial burden of the emergency, then get right back on track once it is past, paying off your debts. So, once you do pay off your debts, what then? You can save all their money. You are debt free. Can you stay debt free forever?

You must remember the number one reason that created those debts in the first place.

It was the Capitalistic Free Enterprise system in America. What? Yes, all companies have unlimited freedom to market their products. And they do it through advertising across all media platforms. This means that from childhood to becoming adults, you are bombarded on a daily basis with advertising....on TV, in newspapers and magazines, the internet, billboards and numerous other places.

By the time most of us are in college, or out in the workplace, we have been systematically brainwashed to want to accumulate "stuff."

We want to buy stuff...shop, spend, buy....keep up with the Joneses and make sure we have as much stuff as they do. We are programmed with the automatic mindset to buy, buy, BUY. Believe or not, many of us have developed a deeply ingrained habit to get more and more stuff, even if we have to go in debt to get it.

Using the second method, or Cash Flow Management, you will pay off debt and save every month at the same time. This could be harder, but it could also be better. Why? Because it will take longer to eliminate all of your debt, but you will have that emergency cash savings account if you need it as a security blanket. Continuing to buy stuff while implementing this method might come more naturally to the American way of living.

It's similar to running a business. You must do many of the same things each and every month to make a profit when you run a business. This holds true with running your household, as well, in order to create more savings and net worth.

So which method is best? Both are good. You should go with the one that best fits your 'fixed or growth mindset'. Each person will have to decide what is best for their household income plan.

Let's go over each of the three systems and how it can work for you, beginning with Debt Management.

What kind of debt do Americans incur? More than you might imagine. 96% of graduate students carry an average of six credit cards. Graduate business students accumulate the most credit card debt, with an average balance of $11,585, and that figure does not include student loans.

The percentage of Americans who live paycheck to paycheck is about 70%, and 63% worry about money. 20% of workers wouldn't make their next mortgage, utility, or credit card payments if they missed a paycheck.

Statistics suggest that finances play a critical role in 80% of all divorces. In fact, this issue seems to be the number one or two reason that marriages fail.

The longer Americans are in debt, the harder it is to break free. They must have a definite plan in place in order to get out of debt.

What would it mean to you and your family to be debt free? What amount of wealth accumulation could be made from the interest you pay to credit card companies?

Here is an idea for you: Why not act as your own bank and pay yourself the loan payment, thus saving the interest? Then have it credited to one of your savings or investment accounts.

For example, if you average $5,000 a year for twenty years in interest payments, you would pay a minus -$100,000. If you invested the $5,000 a year into a long-term, twenty-year investment that averaged 10%, you would have $286,000 plus the $100,000 interest savings to equal almost a half million dollars.

> Figure your interest savings using the Rule of 72, and you will be amazed at your new wealth.

The debts we are talking about are consumer type loans—loans or credit card charges that make no investment return to you. Most of these debts are created because something was purchased that probably was not needed.

Business and real estate loans, on the other hand, can leverage your money to produce gains and profits. Loans can get the equipment, inventory, or employees to make more money than the loan amount. Get it?

How do you pay off all your debts so that you can pay yourself the interest? The first step is to write out a debt management plan that is separate from your total financial plan.

If you plan to stay in the same house for the rest of your life, then you can include your mortgage in your debt plan. I will show you in a later chapter how to sell your home every two to five years for a profit and invest in a newer, bigger home.

A mortgage is a debt, but if managed and leveraged correctly, it can produce an excellent return. Remember, your plan is to become financially independent or better.

Depending on your interest, you must decide whether to pay more toward your mortgage or toward paying off the high interest on a credit card or loan. Interest will also help determine if you should live in your home for the rest of your life or buy a new home after a few years. I believe that once you get on track toward your financial goals, you will want to invest in a new house every two to five years.

Now, let's focus on paying off the total credit card debt and loans in a reasonable time period, one you can live with.

The first step is to figure out how much more a family can pay a month toward debt balances. The money will come from their cash flow monthly plan.

Let's say that you discover you can cut some of the dining out and entertainment expenses you incur each month. You pledge to put an extra $200 a month toward paying off your debts. You should then set up a plan that will help you pay off one debt at a time, until all of the debts are paid in full.

You need to look at the debts with the highest interest rates and the highest monthly payments.

You could be debt free (not including mortgage) in a few years!

Think about it! You could be totally debt free in five to ten years. Once all debts are paid except for the mortgage, you would have two choices for your mortgage:

Pay it off based on the same plan shown above for debts, and then pay your debt payments to the mortgage, and it would be paid off in full within a few short years.

Your second choice would to leverage your current savings/investment plan of using the debt payments, invest the money in other accounts and diversify your assets. You could divide up the payments (prior debt payments) into four investments per month equally, or any other percentage that works for you.

So the question is: should you pay off the mortgage or put your money into different investments? The answer depends on your total financial plan as well as your goals. If you pay off the mortgage, you will need to make all savings payments to the mortgage for several years. If one of your goals is to buy a new home, you could sell the house now and invest the difference in a new home. Alternatively, you could finance the new home with the least amount of down payment, and then invest the difference.

The question is: Can you make more money (or return) by continuing to pay a mortgage while investing your monthly savings into other investments? Based on historical returns, you should be able to make more returns in other investments than you would by paying off your mortgage.

This is cash you could use for other investments, including real estate or your own business. The more "liquid" you are, the more opportunities and the more leverage you have for additional investments.

There is a second method for getting out of debt. If you qualify, you can pay off your debts faster than you could use the first plan. You leverage your qualified retirement plan to pay off your debts. Your retirement plan must have a loan provision for this plan to work.

While there are others, the two main types of retirement plans that could have a loan provision are 401(k) plans and 403(b) plans, but other types might, too.

A 401(k) is a private sector retirement plan, while a 403(b) is a public sector retirement plan. The public sector plans are for educators and non-profit organizations.

By having a loan provision, you can borrow very cheaply from your retirement account and use that loan to pay off your high-interest loans. You might have to do this a few times to pay off all your debts.

There are two components needed to make this system work. First, you take a loan from your retirement plan at 6% (for example) and since you are using your retirement account as the collateral, you make interest on your money, say 3%. So in fact the loan is costing you 3 % to pay off 15%, 19%, and believe it or not 27%, credit cards balance.

Second, it gets better. If you make your 401k the conduit to pay all your loans and debts, then you would want to have a 401k (403b) balance to borrow. If you understand that if you are contributing $200 a month to your retirement account and you are in the 25% tax bracket, then you have leveraged the tax savings for loan payments.

You save $62 in taxes to contribute $200 to your retirement plan. If you had not saved the $200 through your retirement plan, then you would have to put away $262 away, pay IRS the $62, and save the $200. By using this method, you have an extra $62 to help pay your debts, courtesy of the IRS.

Use that amount to pay all your high percent credit card debts and other loans.

If you have money in your 401(k) or 403(b) plan, but have not yet maximized your contribution allowed by the IRS, you should actively work on doing so. We will talk about all tax plans & retirement plans later in this book. You don't need to be an Einstein to figure out how to borrow low interest and pay off high interest debt off.

We have covered the Debt System; now let's go over the Savings System & Cash Flow System. While we have covered cash flow and savings in prior chapters, there is still quite a bit more ground to cover.

First, you will have to learn and understand each of the three parts of Capital Management. Once you do, you will basically be doing the same thing every month. This can be boring and not very exciting, but it builds wealth, which is exciting.

It will take discipline to do this every month and this is where you develop a 'growth mindset'.

Cash flow now is simple, because it is about how to use all the income you have available every month and then allocate your living expenses, debt, and savings. This takes work and patience.

When we talk about savings accounts, which ones do we put our income into? There are many, many choices. Remember, this is the USA---home of the free enterprise system.

We will cover a little bit here and more in subsequent chapters. For now, you may have to take what you can get or understand. For example, if your employer is doing a matching contribution into a 401k, then you should match the contribution. If not, then you will be throwing money away.

Since you are just starting, you will need to put some of your money into short-term savings accounts and money market accounts. Then, after you have an emergency account which is equal to three to six months of your income, you can put money into longer-term accounts.

Long-term savings & investment accounts, historically, will make you more earnings or return. There are many accounts for you to choose from. You will have to consider how long-term investment accounts are taxed. There are several ways an investment can be taxed. Some are taxed the year you make earnings on them, and some later on. And some you pay less tax or tax-free.

Most Americans have their savings & investments in Taxable and Tax Deferred (Postponed) accounts. Taxable means they are taxed in the year they earn. Tax-Deferred are mostly retirement accounts and the tax is paid when they take it out, hopefully in retirement.

Then we have to consider the risk of each investment account, because our money mindset will dictate what accounts to invest in. It doesn't take long for a person to figure out that short-term savings account, CD's, and money market accounts are safe & liquid. Why? Because that is all they know, and their fixed money mindset tells them too.

Long-term investments historically have produced much higher returns. They carry a risk of down markets and losing money in some years. But if you invest for the long term and keep the money in those accounts, the returns are higher.

We will discuss more about long-term investments in a later chapter on the Market. To conclude the part of the savings method, it is a major tragedy for Americans to invest in short-term accounts when they are in there 20's or 30's, because this was the absolute best time to invest in long-term accounts. By the time they reach their 50's or 60's, and now understand how long-term accounts make earnings, this is the time to become more conservative.

This is why we need 'Money Management' courses in high school, and not as an elective. These three methods of Money (Capital) Management, is just the right course for them. It has been shown that just ten hours of money management training can be the difference in managing a household and getting out of debt, as well as not getting into debt.

For those than attend college, a similar course and a second course (required) on long-term investments and financial independence. Our young adults can enter the workforce and finally know what to do with their first paycheck and their last. Can you just imagine what our country would be like today, if all our government officials had taken these required courses?

When we talk about savings accounts, which ones do we put our income into? There are many, many choices. Remember, this is the USA---home of the free enterprise system.

We will cover a little bit here and more in subsequent chapters. For now, you may have to take what you can get or understand. For example, if your employer is doing a matching contribution into a 401k, then you should match the contribution. If not, then you will be throwing your money away.

Since you are just starting, you will need to put some of your money into short-term savings accounts and money market accounts. Then, after you have an emergency account which is equal to three to six months of your income, you can put money into longer-term accounts.

Long-term savings & investment accounts, historically, will make you more earnings or return. There are many accounts for you to choose from. You will have to consider how investment accounts are taxed as there are many different ways. Some are taxed the year you make earnings on them, and some later on.

The Capital Management system now becomes, through routine practice and of course discipline, a simple question of which accounts do you send money to every month.

By doing this every month, you will start to increase your net worth and your assets, while eliminating your liabilities. It is a slow process that never seems fast enough. But if you can develop stick-to-it-ive-ness, you will reap rich rewards!

CHAPTER SIX

My Own Master Mind Team

A Master Mind Team is composed of different advisors that the investor or the family has chosen to guide and advise them on financial, tax, business, risk management, legal and other matters. Believe it or not, most Americans do not have a team of advisors.

You have already learned that the majority of Americans are not wealthy or financially independent. Now you know why.

What do you think is the number one reason that the majority of US citizens don't have a Master Mind Team? If you said it's due to the cost or expense of each advisor, you would be partially correct---but that's just the tip of the iceberg. Scratch the surface and you get to deeper reasons.

Many of us have learned from our parents and others that all advisors charge a lot of money for their services. If you sit down with any advisor, they will charge you a lot of money, right? You are scared that if you did consult an advisor of some sort, you would end up spending money you can't afford.

That's understandable, of course. But, the real problem is the 'financial mindset', or the 'fixed habit' of making money decisions on your own. You have a set-in-stone perception that if you save expenses on money advice or investments, you will have more money.

Ask yourself this question: Do you really believe that? Or is it that you have that perception because you don't really understand much about money and investments?

If you think you will be wasting your hard earned money to have advisors help you spend it wisely, this is your own 'fixed habit'. It is your mindset and maybe it seems that you just can't help yourself or change your way of thinking. But you can!

In fact, if you are serious about wanting to become a millionaire---you will absolutely have to change that mindset!

If, at this point, if you are getting a little tired of reading about the 'mindset', this should throw up a red flag and tell you it's a problem you need to work on post haste. Your mindset will control whether or not you are able to become wealthy. If it is negative and you have convinced yourself you'll never be financially independent; you must change it to the positive as soon as possible or you won't ever become wealthy.

If the cost of hiring a Master Mind professional was truly the reason most people don't do it, then why do 90% of us have little or no net worth? Why are there so many of these professionals in America?

You may have heard the story many times about how, in buying the cheapest products or services, you usually get what you pay for. You probably have some firsthand knowledge of buying cheap products and being disappointed. What happens sometimes when you sacrifice quality for price? You wind up spending more in the long run because the cheap, shoddy products malfunction or don't work right from the get-go, so you then must turn around and purchase a replacement product.

Another point to consider is that you will almost always pay more for things if you have to put them on your credit card because you don't have the cash to outright pay for it.

It's a never ending, very vicious cycle of middle class America---always paying more; while the people with a higher net worth pay cash, saving a lot of money.

Think about this comparison of a higher net worth person and a 'fixed money mindset' person. In this scenario, they each buy the same product. The one with a higher net worth pays $750 for the widget, and pays with cash, which often means a lower price from the merchant, money talks.

The other one buys with a credit card and pays $1000 instead of $750 because of *not* paying cash. Plus, that person pays the interest on the $1000 for three years, which equals $1450. It all shakes out to a savings straight across the board of $700 for the higher net worth person who plunked down cash. Figuring in a modest amount of interest on that money means a total of $800 saved. Over time, you can imagine how that builds the net worth!

Getting back to our Master Mind Team costs and expenses, if you have all your financial records up to date you would see that advisors actually make you money. Having a team of professionals who understand the ins and outs of money will save you money while helping you add to your net worth.

Looking at it from that viewpoint....it isn't a question of whether or not you can afford to have this team of advisors, but can you afford not to have it?

If you researched every public corporation and private businesses, as well, that are profitable; you would see that they have a team of advisors. Many companies have two sets of advisors, one set on the payroll of the company as fulltime employees, and the other set as contractors to the company.

It's almost a matter of simply taking a lesson from these successful corporations and businesses and following their examples. Do what they do!

Do I have to bring up the 'fixed mindset' again? You have to start the change that will morph from an established routine to a habit. While nobody can deny that there are some unethical advisors out there, these are the exceptions; not the rule. To protect yourself, interview each advisor, just as those big companies do before they hire a team to advise them about their finances.

You should plan on doing interviews during your one hour a week planning session. You can conduct the interviews by phone, internet-email, or face-to-face. Make a list of the advisors or team members that you think you may need. Then, work on getting at least three professionals per category. Set up the interviews and remember.....you are the CEO of your home business and your business is to accumulate assets & wealth!

What are some of the ways a Master Mind Team of advisors can help you? The name 'Master Mind Team' comes from the book "Think and Grow Rich." Written in the 1920's, it is still a much read classic today. The author, Napoleon Hill, wrote the book over a ten year period while he was traveling across America and interviewing millionaires.

What did Napoleon Hill want to come out of the interviews with millionaires? He wanted to know how they thought and whether there were common traits and goals. One of the common traits he discovered in all of these wealthy people is that all the 'Millionaires' had a Master Mind Team of advisors.

The people he interviewed were very good at making money from their occupation or business. But they figured out quickly that this is not the same thing as being good at making money from their money. It's the same today. Many Americans are good at making a salary or income on what they know how to do, but not good at making that money work for them after they have made it.

Again, it's that stupid 'money mindset' that we cannot shake. It's like saying that you don't need to see a doctor or an attorney because you can do what they do.

Here are several ways that a Master Mind Team of advisors can help you:

- Save you a lot of dollars in taxes every year.
- Save you interest charges.
- Increase your portfolio return.
- Save your family money in probate expenses.
- Increase your Asset protection from lawsuits.
- Provide income & capital if not able to work.
- Decrease your risk of down markets.
- Provide more benefits for your company.
- Set up a way to pay for your kids college.
- Save you hours of time to do other things.

Turn around 360 degrees and start to find your team. They will make you money, save you money, and protect your money & assets.

What advisors should you have on your team? Every person or family is different and you will interview team members that you need until you have developed a 'growth habit' and a 'financial mindset' that is building & creating assets & wealth.

Let's look at some potential team members:

- Financial Planner/Advisor
- Tax Professional
- Attorney
- Real Estate Agent
- Insurance Agent

- Computer Consultant
- Marketing Consultant
- Business Consultant

Some of these professionals you recognize and some you may not. You may be thinking that you know how to use a computer and don't need a consultant. Remember your arch enemy; the fixed mindset before you make a decision on this. Now, let's describe each one in a little more detail and look at the services your future Master Mind Team could offer you.

Tax-Professional—This advisor might be a CPA or a Tax-Preparer, or a Bookkeeper with the experience to do tax returns, your payroll, as well as how to file business tax returns; plus what deductions or benefits you qualify for.

Before we describe the rest of your team, let's discuss business ownership for a minute. This is because many people can save, invest, and create net worth without 'owning' or running a business. You may not even want to own or run a business, because you like your job. Maybe you don't want a business because you have seen a lot of failures, so you don't like the risk of owning a business.

If you aren't interested in becoming a business owner, you can continue your current employment and make an income....invest in stocks, real estate, and tax-plans; without having a business. A lot of people have created large net worth's while being a 'W-2 employee.'

The point here is that a business is the fourth opportunity in America to create assets for producing net worth and financial independence. America's 'free enterprise' system makes it an unlimited opportunity for all of its citizens. Remember, get on to the 'growth mindset', and don't believe anything negative you might have heard about being a business owner. Research and find out for yourself, so that you can make an informed decision instead of merely taking someone else's word for it.

We will cover 'business equity' versus business ownership later in the book and you will discover the real reason that you might want to get into your own business.

Financial Planner/Advisor—Can advise you & your family on many parts of your planning process and help you to set the right goals, save on taxes, save on interest, protect some of your assets, recommend investments & portfolios, money & debt management, manage your investments, provide insurance recommendations, and guide you in planning your estate for your beneficiaries and setting up trusts.

Attorney—First of all you may require the services of more than one attorney, depending on what your financial goals are and what type of legal documents you need. You may need a business attorney that specializes in business instruments, and another attorney to provide estate planning and the required legal documents.

Real Estate Professional—You will most certainly purchase a house, and in fact you may purchase more than three homes in your lifetime, including building a home. But because you fully understand the 'growth mindset', you may purchase eight homes in your lifetime. Even though the average person in the US purchases three homes in their lifetime, you understand the big tax breaks that IRS gives you to build wealth & net worth when you buy and sell your house. You want a Real Estate Professional that understands your financial goals and growth mindset to help you plan the right time to buy and sell real estate. In addition, a real estate agent can help you when you are ready to invest in rental properties, commercial real estate, and even raw land.

Insurance Agent—A good insurance agent can protect your assets from losses and provide liability protection for lawsuits & claims. Here is another example of how it may be desirable to have more than one agent on your Advisory Team. Many insurance agents specialize in different insurance products and many financial planners are insurance planners as well. While we could say that all insurance agents are able sell a lot of the same products, you will also have insurance specialists. For example, you may have an agent that only handles your Property & Casualty insurance, like auto insurance, property coverage, liability, and commercial insurance. You might also have an agent that handles medical, group insurance, life & disability insurance & Long-Term Care. Other specialists may handle insurance policies for business owners for succession planning, retirement planning, employee benefits, and estate planning.

Computer or IT Consultant—Once again, you can use a professional that has knowledge of both hardware & software, and internet. But there are specialists for each, so you can opt to go with two consultants. You want to choose a team member that can provide recommendations for purchasing hardware as to size, memory, speed, programs, connections, brand names, power, and cost. When something goes wrong with your computer or computers, or servers, you need someone that knows how to fix them fast, and not someone that will charge you while they are learning themselves.

We don't expect them to know everything on computer technology because it changes so fast, but you don't need consultants or advisors who will charge you while they are still learning, themselves.

We will cover Internet Specialists under Marketing and Business Consultants. Some of you will have an Internet Team Member as well as a Computer, Marketing, and Business Consultant.

**

Danger--don't do what the majority of Americans do and that includes the educated ones. 'Never say Never'. 'I don't have to worry about some of the Master Mind Team Professionals because I will not need them for my simple wealth creation plan'. You are back to the 'fixed mindset' and not the 'growth mindset'. The primary goal & purpose is to build & create net worth. That is the end in mind, not which types or ways to do it. If you grow your mindset, they will come.

**

Marketing Consultant—this type of consultant can help you increase your sales & profits by providing you with more outlets to reach more customers. A Marketing Consultant today will recommend methods of getting more contacts, more prospects, and more customers both online & offline. A Marketing Consultant does not have to be an Online or Social Media expert to know the end results of using online social media. An Internet marketing expert would know all about how to use Social Media, such as Linked In and Facebook.

Business Consultant—Many business owners, or should I say new business owners, would not consider a business consultant or a marketing consultant simply because they have little capital to work with. Limited Capital is one of the reasons business fail. But, if you include business consultant fees in your business plan (and don't leave home without it) from the beginning, then you are planning a 'growth model'. A business consultant can help with even the most basic procedures for owning & running a business. The basic items are the ones the new business owner often tries to skip in order to be successful faster.

A Business Consultant will be able to provide you with a business system that will help run the business systematically every month or week, or day. Additionally, the business consultant can provide recommendations on hiring people, setting up the sales process, bookkeeping methods, reporting, advertising & public relations, and what it takes to make profits.

We could have written an entire chapter on each one of the Master Mind Team members, but what is most important to you now is to start the process of interviewing your future team. The other thing for you to know is that just because some of your friends or acquaintances did not use the Master Mind model doesn't mean that you can't.

We already know the number of Americans that are still on the 'fixed mindset' or the 'fixed habit' of taking action every day with their money.

But, if they fall into that majority who has not acquired a high net worth---whoever said they were right?

CHAPTER SEVEN

My Own Asset Protection Plan

As we have said throughout this book, you can achieve your financial and wealth goals through proper pre-planning.

It's true.

You can become financially independent by taking action on your personal financial blueprint. Our next step is to look at ways to protect your net worth. It would be pretty awful to work and work and build your net worth to an amount far beyond your dreams, only to have it stripped away because you failed to protect it.

There are several ways to protect your assets. Some of these things are easy and some require more time. Some will require new fees. The fees may seem 'high' to you, but if so, it's only because you have not paid them before.

Remember that 'fixed' mindset that we all tend to have and don't let it derail you! That negative mindset is self defeating if you don't banish it and replace it with something better and more positive.

The good news is that you probably have some experience and have most likely already done a bit of minor asset protection. For example, you probably have insurance to protect you against financial losses from auto accidents, or house fires, or a major medical expense, or even your death.

We will cover more on insurance later.

One of the best ways to protect assets is to use the pyramid shaped design that lists all the different strategies. In other words, the bottom part will be the biggest or widest part of the pyramid, which means this would serve as your foundation.

You will start at the bottom with the foundation part and protect all you can at that point. Then you will check that part off and go to the next level of asset protection. You can also create your own format using all the strategies that will be covered.

As you move up the scale of a higher net worth, it creates a whole new problem in that there are plenty of "predators" out there who are only too happy to take your assets off your hands. Since the majority of Americans have never reached those wealth goals, asset and wealth portfolios are thought of as something only for the "rich."

However, rest assured that any degree of savings, investments, business & real estate ownership can be taken from you by just one lawsuit. Only one. That's all it takes. You need to protect your wealth from anyone who wants to take it from you in a lawsuit. It doesn't matter if it is caused by an accident, negligence or even a minor error.

There are numerous strategies for building a "financial fortress" around your assets. If you have built your "Master Mind" team of advisors, then you would ask your advisor attorney for help. This is absolutely critical.

If you doubt it, consider the fact that someone is sued in America every minute of every day, 365 days a year.

In fact, of all the lawsuits filed worldwide, more than 90% are filed in the United States.

We will review several types of asset and wealth protection strategies. The more strategies you set up, the more protection you will have for your assets. Never forget that the wealth you spent so many years and so much hard work accumulating can be taken from you overnight, in the blink of a eye. It might be easier to make the money than it is to keep it. As your wealth increases, your enemies or demons will also multiply.

Your best action is to meet with your advisor attorney and get each legal document written and in place for your protection. The majority of middle-income Americans and even some wealthy ones hesitate to meet with an attorney because of the fees. This is another mindset you need to conquer. It could cost you a lot if you don't set up your "fortress" properly.

The British have a wise saying about trying to save money in ways that could actually cost you money in the long run. They call it being "penny wise and pound foolish." Basically, this is the case with not wanting to spend a little money to consult with a trained professional attorney when it could cost you a LOT of money if you don't.

If you still are thinking about the cost of the legal fees, you may still have the 'fixed' mindset of being strapped for cash and therefore hesitant to spend money on an attorney. Ask your Advisory team for recommendations and then work on your annual budget.

Not every asset protection plan will involve hiring an attorney. There are several asset protection strategies to consider and that will require appropriate action. It will be up to you to make decisions on which to implement.

Let's look at a list of the possible asset protection strategies. You can use the following and start from the foundation or base and move up:

Asset Protection Model

Insurance Protection:

Insurance, believe it or not, can protect a good portion of your assets. This is why we have so many insurance companies & agents in America. Many agents sell the lowest price coverage because that is what so many people want. But, this is not always the best strategy if you want to protect your assets.

In a nutshell, you need the best coverage you can possibly afford in order to protect your net worth. Consult with your Advisor team on all the types of coverage you need.

Now, let us look at a menu of required insurance to protect your assets and net worth. Remember that if maximum insurance is recommended, it doesn't mean you have to spend a lot of money. You have to also consider your budget and the risks involved.

Liability Insurance is usually the easiest and often the most overlooked asset protection for your vehicle. Although many people cling to a "the cheaper, the better" mindset, it is preferable to increase your coverage. Experts would say that your auto liability insurance limits should be increased to the maximum or highest you can afford.

You should increase your **homeowner's liability insurance** coverage to the maximum limits, as well. While you're at it, make sure you have replacement value protection on your home and its contents.

If you have a home business, ecommerce or otherwise, or a commercial business location, this requires separate **business liability protection** and fire insurance. In addition, an Umbrella liability policy is recommended, in the event that a claim exceeds your liability limits.

Medical insurance is a priority for yourself and family. You don't want to have a medical claim of $100k paid from your assets, or a judgment issued against you for a huge sum of money. Medical debts account for approximately 60% of the bankruptcies in the United States and one long stay in the hospital could wipe out your savings and entire net worth without good insurance to cover these exorbitant costs. Medical costs have been increasing at a higher rate than regular inflation.

Life Insurance is payable to your beneficiary or to the bank or mortgage company upon your death. This is what most people understand about life insurance. But, the best use of Life Insurance is to replace 'you', or your 'spouse', or business 'partner' as an asset that is creating income or earnings. This is called the 'human value'. While no money in the world would replace you as a husband or a father of your children if you have any, there is a maximum economic value. That economic value will hopefully increase over time, so you will probably need to increase the benefit amount as your earnings and net worth increase.

So, the question is this: how much life insurance should a person be insured for? There are several ways to calculate the right amount. One fast and easy way to arrive at a ballpark figure is to divide your total annual income by 3%; $60,000/3% equals $2 million dollars.

This means that you are worth at least $2 million dollars as an 'asset' value, financially speaking. From this amount you factor in whether or not your spouse will continue to work, the amount of your liquid assets, whether or not any debts will be paid off at your death and your life expectancy. The figure you come up with after these calculations is the amount of life insurance you need.

Many people don't think of themselves as assets, but they are almost always the greatest asset in creating their own net worth. The other major consideration for life insurance is the replacement value of the person to a business entity, such as a corporation.

The next type of insurance product is called DI insurance, or **Disability Income insurance**. This insurance is to replace your salary or income if you should become disabled and can no longer work or be productive. It can replace only earned income, not investment income. You can ordinarily qualify for 60 to70 percent of your salary or earned income.

If you are an employee of a company, you may have DI available to you through your job. It may be either a short-term benefit (six months or less coverage), or long-term benefits of up to five years or more, or even both. If you own a business, you will have to seek out the right DI for you and your business.

Long-Term Care Insurance or LTC is one of the newest types of insurance coverage even though it has been available for 30 years. One of the major reasons that more Americans want LTC insurance is the increase in longevity in the United States. We could probably say that all of us will need some sort of long-term care, even if it's only for a week before we die. The major reason that you would want to purchase LTC insurance is to protect your assets from going to zero.

According to US statistics the average long-term care is about three years. The cost of LTC insurance can be high, depending if you are age 50 or age 70 when you apply for it. LTC is considered to be care in a nursing home, or home-health care, or in some private retirement homes.

Contrary to popular belief, long-term health care is not covered by health insurance or Medicare. Medicare is your health insurance at age 65 and later. Medicaid is LTC coverage basically for those that have no assets.

Since you want to protect your assets because you are creating net worth and wealth, your best bet is LTC insurance, or you can opt to self-fund with your assets. LTC insurance covers what medical insurance will not cover.

Medical insurance will not cover what is referred to as the "activities of daily living" or ADL. ADL includes bathing, dressing, toileting, transferring, eating, and continence. LTC insurance will pay usually when a person cannot do two or more activities on the ADL list.

As you can see, there are plenty of insurance coverage types to protect your assets and net worth. That is why it is the foundation and the biggest part of the blocks that form the pyramid.

Now we'll move up one level to the second asset protection block, QRP.

Qualified Retirement Plans (QRP), are considered good asset protection vehicles because they are protected from the claims of a beneficiary's creditors under the federal law known as The Employees Retirement Income Security Act of 1974 (ERISA).

Qualified means that the retirement plan is approved by the Internal Revenue as a legal plan for retirement accumulation.

A QRP might be sponsored by your employer. It could be a 401k, a Pension, or a Profit Sharing Plan. If you have no retirement plan through your employer, you may qualify for an IRA or a 403b plan.

Many retirement plans become the largest asset in a person's total portfolio. The other benefit of a retirement plan is that you are able to contribute more leveraged savings into the plan after taxes. We will discuss the other benefits of 'tax plans' in a later chapter, in greater detail.

There are also trusts and a variety of good retirement plans that contain what is called a "spendthrift provision." A spendthrift provision prohibits the beneficiary of the trust from alienating or assigning his or her interest in the trust, and also prohibits the creditors of a beneficiary from invading the trust to satisfy their claims against the beneficiary.

Most states have passed statutes that protect retirement plans from the claims of creditors. There are other types of retirement plans that are protected from the claims of creditors. These plans are called NQP-Non Qualified plans. This type of plan means that the asset is protected, just like the QRP plans. The major difference between the two is that the contributions into these NQP have no tax deduction benefit.

Examples of these NQP types are Permanent Life Insurance Plans and Tax-Deferred Annuities. More discussion on these types of plans will be covered in the 'tax plans' chapter.

Business Entity can serve as an asset protection vehicle if it is the right type of entity. The corporation entity is regarded as one of the best.

You have probably heard of the saying, "piercing the corporate veil." This is what is meant by it, as it is extremely difficult to get to the assets in a lawsuit.

Other entities that can be set up, either as additional business entities or by themselves include the following:

- Sub-S corporations
- LLC-Limited Liability Companies.

Sit down with your advisory team members, which may include an attorney, an accountant and a financial advisor, to discuss the best entity for your business.

Trusts are the next level of protection.

Trusts can protect assets from creditors and lawsuits, and also protect your family from paying attorney fees and probate costs. Trusts may include 'powers of attorney' and 'medical directives', which can also protect your assets if you are no longer able to make legal decisions.

We will discuss two types of trusts which are probably the most used. That being said, bear in mind that there are many other trusts available, depending on your goals.

The Revocable Living Trust – A revocable living trust can provide you and your family with the following benefits:

- Allows the avoidance of probate
- Remains a private estate planning document in life and death
- Provides savings on estate taxes
- Control of your assets that are owned by your living trust
- Designate who will manage your affairs upon your incapacity

- Protects wealth for your loved ones from creditors & divorce
- Offers much flexibility & hard to contest
- Reduces the likelihood of having unintended heirs
- Is legal and enforceable in every state
- Avoids multiple states probate with a living trust
- Is easy to maintain

This living trust can replace your will, which is subject to probate and is public record. The living trust is the primary trust for yourself and your family. You can add many additional trusts. Visit with your team attorney and find out about all the different types of trusts.

The Irrevocable Life Insurance Trust–The ILIT, as it is called, is the second type of trust to define. As you can tell just from the name, it has insurance and it is irrevocable, which means that unlike the Living Trust, once you make an ILIT it cannot be changed. But that is not a negative at all, because if it can't be changed it has some good tax & planning benefits for your family.

An ILIT is set up to carry assets. In most cases, this is a life insurance policy that is in the ILIT or owned by the ILIT. There is a cash value asset in the life insurance policy, but the biggest benefit it contains is the death benefit. Since it is owned by the ILIT trust, then upon death the proceeds go to the ILIT (trust). This means that no estate taxes were paid from the death benefit amount. This is a good thing.

The two major benefits of the ILIT trust with the death benefit proceeds are:

1. *To pay any estate taxes that are due to the estate*
2. *To provide income for your spouse and children, or family*

You don't need a high net worth to set up an ILIT trust. The majority of Americans have not set up an ILIT trust. This may be because they don't believe they need it and it necessitates paying an attorney's fee.

But, families with children---and especially when either or both spouses earn a good income--- should consider a ILIT trust.

When a parent dies while any children are still young, the ILIT can provide for the income loss of that parent. This could include income for the children all the way through college graduation. It can also provide income for a spouse up to a certain age, or even for life.

When you consider the present value of you and/or your spouse's income for the next 20 years, the cost of setting up an ILIT trust is very reasonable and imminently worthwhile.

The last asset protection strategy that we will cover is called the **'Family Limited Partnership' (FLP)**. This doesn't mean it's the last of all asset protection strategies. So, meet with your team attorney for more information about other protection strategies.

A Family Limited Partnership is a limited partnership in which the general and the limited partners are family members. The FLP offers:

- Asset protection
- Protection from income taxes
- Possible reduction of potential estate taxes at death

An FLP can reduce the size of your estate by allowing you to give majority shares in the partnership to family members, while still providing you with 100% control over your assets. You, as the general partner, are in complete control over all aspects of the business or investments of the partnership.

At what point in your life should you consider taking action to protect your assets?

Remember, even if you don't have a net worth of tangible assets, you should take care of yourself as your primary and biggest asset. As to the rest of your tangible assets, it's up to you to determine when your assets should be protected.

You should make a list of all the documents that you have, and then add to the list the ones you will consider later. Here is a sample:

Asset Protection and Estate Planning Documents

_____ Birth Certificate

_____ Marriage Certificate

_____ Military Discharge Papers

_____ Divorce Papers

_____ Passport

_____ Insurance Policies

_____ Stocks and Bonds

_____ Investment Statements

_____ Deeds and Mortgages

_____ Bank-Credit Union Statements

_____ Titles

_____ Wills

_____ Living Trusts

_____ Business Agreements

_____ Power of Attorney

_____ ILIT Trust & other trusts

_____ Tax Returns

_____ Family Limited Partnership

_____ Retirement-Pension Plans

CHAPTER EIGHT

My Own Money 'Market' Plan

You can be assured that the United States of America is the home of the best free enterprise and capital system in the world. In addition, the US 'Stock Market' is the largest in the world by a huge margin.

Through the American system, the stock market has become the 'money market' center for all Americans and the rest of the world. The 'Market' for savings and investments includes all that is available for any person to invest or save.

The 'market' is the first of the four asset categories where you will accumulate, save and invest your money.

The other three asset categories are:

1. *Tax plans*
2. *Real estate*
3. *Business equity*

Your first choice should be to 'take action' and save money. Reading and learning about investments and assets is great.....but taking action to save money is even better.

So, how does the average American feel about the market? How do most US citizens feel about how they invest in the market? For the majority of people, it is still the same 'fixed mindset' that has been learned throughout life. Most people don't invest in the equities market, or else they save in conservative debt instruments.

Let's look at what kind of investment options are available in the market and how to select these options, based on their risk.

There are thousands of investment products and portfolios available in the market. Many products are similar, but have a different company name on them. In actuality, there are really only two categories or types of investments in the Market:

1. *Debt investments*
2. *Equity investments*

How much would you like to invest in a 'Debt' investment every month till you turn age 66?

If you have not heard the term 'debt instrument' before, you probably are thinking that you don't invest in debt. But you probably do without realizing it, and you also almost certainly own a few, or many.

Debt Instruments are pledges or notes to YOU.

You will get paid interest or dividends for lending money to the US Government or to Public Corporations in America. But here is where the 'debt' name is changed and you may already have guessed why. Would you invest in US Government Bonds, or Treasury Bills, or Corporate Notes? These are all 'debt instruments'.

When you invest $1,000 into a US Government Bond, you are lending money to the USA and in turn, they will pay you a dividend, or interest. Then, one day in the future, you get your original $1,000 back. Your return is based on the annual dividend.

When you consider investing $5000 in Corporate Bonds, you are lending money to public corporations. But you will also look at Government Bonds, who will probably pay a lower dividend than the Corporations dividend. Why is this, the case? Public companies have to pay more to compete with the US Government.

If you were to look at an average Debt or Bond Chart, you would see that the average dividend or interest line is almost straight. The Government and Corporations want to pay the lowest cost of borrowing money, while staying competitive.

The dividend or interest payment, whether low or high, is what is paid back to the investor, plus the original principle. People invest in bonds because they want a conservative investment, one that pays them an income check. The investor is not concerned with growth of the asset, because there is no growth.

There is no growth of the 'bond instrument', nor is there any participation in the value of the Corporation or Government equity. Not as a bondholder anyway. The investor is in the front line as a creditor if the Public Companies were to go into bankruptcy or close down---or even, heaven forbid---the government, to collect what's owed to them.

Remember, the US Government can only issue debt instruments. They cannot issue stock. Only Public Corporations can issue bonds and sell stocks too. These public corporations need money to grow their business and are willing to pay dividends (interest) and also a percentage of the profits.

Though Bonds have no growth, investors have bonds to diversify their portfolio. They like bonds because they can usually count on the same dividend payment. They use the dividend payment for many financial goals such as monthly income, to pay off a mortgage, to buy a boat, pay for college for their children, and almost any other financial goal.

An example of using bonds for the investor's goals is paying for a mortgage. The home mortgage payment is $1,000 a month or $12,000 a year, and the bond portfolio dividend rate is 4%. Then the investor would have to have $300,000 in that bond portfolio.

It doesn't matter that the investor would have earned more of a return with Stocks, because there are also down markets. The bond earnings are more conservative and of the same amount.

The biggest risk for bond investors is Interest Rate risk and the Business Risk. The business risk is this: if you own bonds on a company such as Enron, then the risk is that the company folds and doesn't pay you. If you invest in a portfolio of bond companies, then that risk is lessened, because you have spread the risk over several companies.

The Interest rate risk is that when interest rates go up, the market value of bonds goes down.

For example, let's say that you bought a bond for $10,000 and decide to sell it while interest rates are high. You may only be able to sell it for $9500.

Why is that?

The reason is that investors can get more interest earnings than bond dividends, and so during these periods of high interest, no one is buying bonds. This is true unless the bonds are cheaper to buy, making their total return competitive with interest rates investments.

The other side of the investment world is a the more exciting side for investors because investors can make a higher return, ten times higher than bonds....even a 100 times higher!

Investing in equities or stocks, as most people invest, also carries more risk than investing in bonds. The major difference in stocks versus bonds is that stocks have a 'growth' value. It is listed on the exchanges as 'market value'. This is the price you can command for your stocks, or equities portfolio. It changes every day, because the demand and supply changes every day.

The concept of 'growth' of an investment and the return of dividends or earnings is sometimes hard to grasp. So, we have come up with an example to show the difference. Many people have talked about stocks and bonds for years, and not known the difference. This might be because they have very little investment in stocks or equities, if any.

Even if it is a simple formula to figure the values of both stocks & bonds, the average American will not grasp it immediately. Unless someone is investing money regularly into both stocks and bonds, they have no 'money mindset' or reason to care about these values. Remember, your mindset doesn't understand yet how to invest or manage money.

There are many ways to compare the differences between stocks and bonds, and some might be too technical. Here is a different kind of example, maybe a little off, but one that you will understand very fast. The example shows how two rental houses would compare.

Rental house B is the bond investment and rental house S is the stock investment. Both houses were bought for cash, and you collect rent on both properties. The rent is income, or dividends. Rental house B brings $500 a month for the next 20 years and is rented continuously.

Rental house S starts out bringing in $500 a month in rent, with periods when it is not rented. But, over the next 20 years, the rent is raised several times on Rental house S, so that at the end of 20 years the rental income has increased to $1000 a month.

Then, at the end of 20 years, you sell both houses. Rent house B is sold for the same price that you paid for it. An investor is thinking that they had 20 years of rental (dividend) income and then got all the principle back, and is excited. Rental house S is sold for three times what the investor paid for the house. In 20 years the rental income (dividend) was four times more than rental house B, because of normal rental (cost of living) increases.

The investor in Rental House S had growth of their rental house, or growth of real estate, which we understand. We also know now that the periods when rental house S was not occupied is referring to times in our economy when the market was down.

So, which rental house would you invest in? You probably will answer rental house S for stocks, right?

But it is during those times of 'No Rent' that our emotions take hold and are apt to control us. If you think that your rental house S is losing money, or will go down in value, you may sell that house and come out making less than rental house B.

Both Stocks and Bonds can be part of your portfolio and still make a good return for you. The example was to illustrate that you can own both types of investments. You would favor one or the other, at different times in your life, because of your emotions.

What are the risks of stocks or equities?

The biggest risk is 'the market' itself. The other risk is 'the business risk'. Business Risk is when you invest in one company or one stock (Enron) and then that business goes belly up and you lose everything you invested. You might have bought all of one stock because you worked for the company or maybe you just liked that particular stock and had high hopes for it. You can eliminate the business risk of losing everything in one fell blow by investing in many companies, through several individual stock purchases, Mutual Funds, ETF's and a diversified portfolio.

The other risk, which is 'market risk', is controlled by the market itself. The causes of 'market risk' tend to be the macro events in our lives. The inflation rate or 'CPI', the value of the dollar, unemployment, interest rates, the deficit, are some of the causes. This means that your portfolio could be worth less one day than the day before.

Your value could continue to go down for several days---even for months or a year. If you were to sell in down markets, you would sell for a loss and because of that, might never buy stocks or equities again.

But if you look at the historical values charts as far back as you want to go, you would see that stocks or equities make the highest returns. You would also see that after the years of 'negative returns', or down years, the following years made positive returns.

We could say that if you own stocks long enough you would always make a positive return, correct? But we can't predict the future, and the day that you are experiencing a down market, your emotions may control you. It doesn't matter about all the historical charts that you have seen. Your portfolio is a negative number, and you think about it.....a lot.

It is always best to know your risk 'tolerance' before you invest!

When you understand risk tolerance, you will already know that your portfolio can have a negative return and won't stress about it over much.

Remember this, too: investing in the Market is investing in the United States of America. We live in the greatest country in the world....a 'Free Enterprise' country. The USA is the youngest, big country in the world (235 years) to make our form of government work.

Other countries are thousands of years old and in case you haven't heard---most have major economic problems without having anywhere close to the amount of capitalization the USA has. This provides proof that our system works. Will it be working in another 100 or 500 years? No one knows.

But, we do know that the free enterprise system is working now and that a person or company can do whatever they want to that is not illegal to make a profit, or a loss, as the system corrects itself.

You cannot expect to make a return of 20% in one year, if you could also have a loss of 20%. We are created to go forward and not backward. To be more positive than negative, to want more than less, to win more than lose, making course corrections along the way.

Let's move on and look at the Market to see what else is available for you to save or invest your money, or your income.

If you understand Bonds (Debt) and Stocks (Equity), then all the other investment products are like stocks & bonds. The differences are that some investments have different periods of maturity, invest in different sectors, some are only international companies, some stocks are large companies, some make changes with the market, some are part of a hybrid or a diversified fund, and so on.

If you invest in an international portfolio of stocks, you are still investing in equities. If you invest in a bond portfolio in the health sector, you have invested in debt instruments for hospitals, medical centers, nursing homes, etc. and this sector still owes you dividends and your principle.

Before you start investing in the market, you may want to know what kinds of investments are available, as well as their return in the past. You can find information almost anywhere on the various types of investments, along with their descriptions and historical returns.

Historical Market Indexes and Historical Market Returns for the 25 year period ending 12/31/2003:

This time period will show the 'Bull' market of the 90s and the subsequent down market in the 2000-2002 time periods.

U.S. 30-day Treasury Bill; an index based upon the average monthly yield of 30-day Treasury Bills. 6.1%

Dow Jones Industrial Average; an unmanaged price weighted index of 30 of the largest, most widely held stocks. 10.8%

Lehman Brother Treasury Bond Index; A total return index of all public organizations of the U.S. Treasury. 10.1%

Lehman Long-Term Credit Bond Index; a total return index of all publicly issued, fixed-rate, non-convertible investment-grade domestic corporate bonds. 10.4%

MSCI-EAFE Equity Index; a total return index in U.S. dollars based or share prices and reinvested gross dividends of approximately 1,100 companies from 20 countries (Europe and Far East). 10.9%

NAREIT REIT; National Association of Real Estate Investment Trust—total return to include all REIT trading on NYSE, and includes real estate investments. 13.0%

NASDAQ—an index of 3,000 OTC issues with an aggregate market value of approximately $500 billion, made up of domestic common stocks. 13.1%

Russell 2000 Growth Index—stocks are selected from 2,000 small companies with higher price-to-book ratios and higher-- forecast growth values. 10.3%

Russell 2000 Value Index—stocks are selected from 2,000 small companies, with lower price-to-book ratios and lower--forecast growth values. 15.8%

S & P 500—an unmanaged market capitalization weighted price index of 500 widely held common stocks listed on the NYSE, AMEX, and the OTC market. 10.3%

Portfolio—made up of 10% of each of the 10 indexes above. 11.7%

Now for your homework, when you are ready to invest and like the looks of a few of the indexes above, research their historical returns for 3, 5, 10 and 20 years to see if you still like that investment index.

The Indexes represent the whole market of that investment category. Most investors will purchase different product or portfolio packages, each with its own brand name. Let's start with the biggest seller of packaged investments, Mutual Funds.

Mutual Funds: A mutual fund is a portfolio containing a large number of stocks and/or bonds. Each mutual fund is managed by a team or manager whose goal is to make a profit from their selection of stocks and bonds. The average mutual fund has about 100 different stocks or bonds in it.

Before the Internet came into being as a full force 'seller' of stocks & mutual funds, the prices for each transaction were higher than today. When a person invests in a Mutual Fund they pay for the mutual fund expenses, so the MF team or manager can buy the 'right' combination of stocks and bonds. The investor can bypass the MF and buy those individual stocks directly from the Market, and on the Internet.

Let's talk about the differences in purchasing a mutual fund or buying 100 stocks. One of the major reasons the American public buys mutual funds today even more than before the internet is the capital to purchase those funds.

You can purchase a MF for as little as $250, or $100 a month, and own a fund that has 100 stocks in the fund.

If you wanted to buy the same 100 stocks that are in the MF, what is the minimum amount of investment? It will probably be between $25,000 and $100,000.

What?!!

Yes, each Stock that is traded has a minimum price. That is why the majority of people, aka investors, purchase mutual funds. While there is less expense in buying stocks, you have to invest more capital.

Many people would bet a million dollars that you are thinking you will try to buy stocks and invest more capital than mutual funds so that you can save on expense charges, correct? But the expense charge is not the only reason to invest in MF or individual stocks.

Will your return be more because you are investing in stocks versus mutual funds?

Almost everyone says yes, including television reporters and money gurus, but you are in the market and anything can happen to a portfolio. In theory, saving investment expenses could make more return, provided that everything else was exactly the same.

The truth is many mutual funds have made more return than a portfolio of stocks. In a mutual fund, the manager or the team can buy & sell stocks all year long. They may only have 50% of the stocks they started with and have the 50% made up of new stocks.

The major reason is to get rid of the 'stocks' that are poor performers, with new stocks to replace them that will do better and hence provide a better return.

If you had been able to invest the minimum into a 100 stocks, and you want to do the same as the MF team, which stocks will you sell and buy?

This takes a lot of work and time, especially if you end up with more of the stocks that don't perform for the year. This is another reason that many people invest in mutual funds.

This is why there are money managers and advisors that will actually buy individual stocks for you and then manage them---sell or buy. For their services, you pay an asset management fee, and can make a higher return than a mutual fund after fees.

We will end the discussion on fees & investment expenses with an example:

Investment G has a total of 2.5% expenses, while Investment H has total fees of 1%. At the end of a three year period, G had a total return of 24% (8% avg per year), and H had a total return of 18% (6% avg per year) after all expenses. Of course the opposite could be true.

The biggest reason that investors do not make a return equal to what the actual Market's or the Indexes return is, or the average mutual fund, is emotions. People get scared and dump their portfolio and put the proceeds into a safe money market. When you have a $100,000 investment and in the course of one short week it goes down to $80,000, you might well panic and decide to bail before you lose all.

You might find out a month later that your fund would have grown to $105k if you had let it be.

Ouch!

Let's move on. We have already mentioned that to decrease the business risk of an investment, you should invest in a portfolio of stocks or companies. This is what a Mutual Fund does, too.

There are many types of Mutual Funds and there are MANY mutual funds, because there are literally unlimited combinations of what stocks and/or bonds go into a mutual fund. This is the reason for doing analysis on your portfolio. You could own 10 mutual funds and you could have the same Public Company in all ten.

Types of Mutual Funds Based on Investment Objective

Asset Allocation: Funds that offer diversification within asset classes and among different asset classes; usually are made up of stocks, bonds, and money market investments.

Balanced Funds: Diversified investments between stocks and bonds; their primary objectives are preservation of capital and moderate growth of income and principal.

Bond Funds: A wide variety of portfolio bond types.

Growth Funds: Funds that concentrate on long-term capital gains and future income, usually no current income; majority in common stocks.

Hedge Funds: Aggressive techniques to include short sales, use of puts and calls, high leverage, for maximum growth.

Income Funds: Invest in securities that usually pay above current rates of return from either dividends or interest; usually a majority of fund portfolio is invested in bonds.

Index Funds: Funds that try to match performance of a market index by creating a portfolio that is similar and try to outperform the market on a risk-adjusted basis.

International Funds: Invest in stocks or bonds of companies that are foreign and have many types, depending on countries and industries.

Money Market Funds: Invest in T-Bills, CDs, and corporate commercial paper, providing current income and relative safety of principal.

Sector Funds: Investments that are made to a particular sector in the market like health care or chemicals, etc.

Specialty Funds: Investments in a single industry, a group of related industries, defined geographical region, or non-security assets.

Tax Exempt Funds: Investments in municipal bonds or other securities that offer tax sheltered income.

Now that you know about Mutual Funds, which ones will you actually invest in? Which one will you invest $1000 and which will you transfer $50,000 to?

Remember, you should research the historical returns of the funds that you are looking to invest in. Will you invest in the ones with the best historical return for 25 years, or 20 years, or 15 years, or 10, 5, or 3 years?

What if the five year return is twice the return of the 25 year return, which one? What if the fund is only five years old and it's return is three times higher than another five year return fund, but that fund is 20 years old?

These are tough questions, and why you will want to understand some of the risk tolerance methods to determine what selection of funds you select.

There are several methods to determine risk, some more technical than the others, and that is why we will discuss a universal method that is conservative in risk determination.

The standard-deviation method is a good way to determine which funds are in line with your risk tolerance. Many investors have purchased funds based on their average return. Sometimes it works for them. Sometimes it doesn't. What if you filled a bucket with boiling hot water and another bucket with ice-cold water, and then put a foot into each bucket?

In theory, you should have an average warm temperature on both feet, right? But in reality, you would still be screaming.

You get the point.

If you invested in a fund that had an average return for the last five years of 10%, and a year later your funds did a minus -6%, you might be mightily upset with the advisor or company you that sold you the fund. But, if you had looked more closely at the historical reports, you would have found the 'standard deviation' was '10'. What the heck does that mean?

One 'standard deviation' equals 68% probability that the fund you have invested in will make between a '0' return and a 20% return. That means that there is a 32% probability that it will be outside that range. For that reason most of the investment industry uses two standard deviations because that equals a 95% probability to be within that range. So let's do a simple standard deviation calculation:

Based on a five year return of 10% and a SD of 20, we could say that there is a 95% probability that your investment return will fall between a minus -10 and +30 percent. There is also a 2.5% chance that the fund will do better than the +30 return, and could do worse than the minus-10 negative return. So if you had known that when you saw your fund take a minus -6%, you wouldn't be as likely to let your emotions get out of hand. If you felt that a -10% loss was just too much for you, you would want an investment that has a lower SD, or less risk.

The 'standard deviation' method of determining risk tolerance may not be the best, but it is a method that most people have never used. The other methods are much more technical than this book will show. Once you have learned the standard deviation method then you can move on to the other types. And best of all, the calculations to determine risk have already been done and are included in most historical reports.

There are a few more investment types and choices we will cover.

The first one, or rather the first two; are called Variable products. The two types of variable products are:

1. *Annuities*
2. *Life Insurance*

These two types of investments have the unique characteristic of encompassing two industries—insurance and securities—in their final products.

Variable Annuity: A variable annuity is a combination of insurance companies' benefits and mutual fund companies' benefits. Its greatest advantage is that no taxes are due on any earnings until you withdraw from the annuity plan. When you withdraw any of your monies, earnings come out before principal and are taxable. If you withdraw before age fifty-nine-and-a-half, there is an additional 10 percent tax penalty.

A Variable Annuity (VA) best benefit is the tax-deferral of earnings, and in many states it is a 'creditor proof' investment. This means that creditors cannot get to those funds to settle any debts owed. Many investors purchase a VA just for the creditor benefit.

Additional benefits can include a guaranteed death benefit of the original principle investment, and a guaranteed income stream for life. After all, that is what insurance companies do best...pay death claims if the participant dies early and pays monthly annuity checks if the client lives a long life.

Once again, the subject of fees & expenses are brought into the decision making of investing in either of the Variable products because they are compared to the expenses & fees of Mutual funds stocks. But, they are different types of investments. Many investors have all types of investments in their portfolio and many just don't care about the other benefits, only the expenses.

There is a perception that investing or buying a VA means that you will receive an income stream for life, like pension plans, except you have no control over the principle. This is a fallacy or myth in the industry. What people are really referring to is 'annuitization', where you take any LUMP SUM amount of money and have the insurance company annuitize it. The money can come from anywhere, such as the VA or from a MF or CD.

But, if you do annuitize your VA, then the income payments will be split from a formula that includes return of principle and the earnings. The return of principle is appealing to many investors because there is not tax paid on the principle part.

Variable Life: The other type of variable product is called Variable Life. Again, there are tax benefits, investment securities options, and a creditor proof portfolio.

This is where it ends, in comparison of a VA. Let's just go over the benefits and then discuss them: A Life Insurance type death benefit from day one; additional optional benefits, loan & withdrawal options, and the option of taking out income on a tax-free basis. Taking income out on a tax-free basis is probably the best benefit and the tax-free part will be covered more in the tax-plans chapter.

The amount of contributions can be any amount to a maximum based on the death benefit chosen. Most Variable Life programs are flexible in the way contributions are made, from a single sum amount to a monthly amount. The money is then invested in several mutual fund type accounts called sub-accounts. From this inside bank of the variable program, it pays for the cost of insurance and all expenses.

Now, we will discuss two investment programs that are similar to the Variable products but at the same time different. These products are called Indexed programs. Again, there is an Indexed Annuity and an Indexed Life Insurance program.

The major difference between the Variable and the Indexed products is that the investment accumulation in the Variable is in the 'stock market'. The Indexed products use a formula based on the market, however the investment is not in the stock market, but in the general funds of a Life Insurance company.

For the most part, Life Insurance Companies are regulated by their state of domicile, and have restrictions on the investments that the insurance company can make. Each state has its own 'State Insurance Board' and they are similar to the FDIC's regulation of banks & financial institutions. Insurance Companies have a certain amount of guaranteed reserves to pay either a death claim or a lifetime income.

Life Insurance companies are regarded as safe type of investments, and the regulators want to make sure that each policy is paid when the American public needs it.

Here is how the Indexed products work:

The majority of the contributions from the investor or policyholder goes into the guaranteed general fund and part of the fund, maybe 10%, is used to buy 'options' on the market. If the options perform for that year, the insurance company gets additional earnings and passes them on to the investor.

On the other hand, if the options did not make a gain, then there is only a cost of the option to the general fund, and the investor receives zero return or a smaller return, but no negative loss.

Index Annuities and Index Life products have been increasing in sales since the first index product came out around the mid 1990's. For now we will just point out a few different benefits from the variable products:

The Indexed Annuity (IA) has enjoyed a good average return without having the money invested in the market and at risk for down markets. There is no loss of principle on the 'zero' earnings years, but the IA has made a 12-14% return in one year, and an average return of 6-8% over a 15-25 year period.

The Index Life Insurance program is very similar to its IA cousin using a similar format of buying options. The major difference is that the investments are not in the market, but in the general funds of the Insurance Company. It does have some additional benefits. One benefit is that in a non-earnings Index year, the insurance company can pay a smaller guarantee versus zero in the IA.

The additional benefit that an Index Life program could have   is an accelerated benefit of the death benefit and a guaranteed lifetime income. Only insurance companies can offer these benefits because of its reserves.

Real Estate Investment Trusts (REIT)

Our next investment to discuss is REIT's for short, or Real Estate Investments Trusts.

REITs are investments that can be invested in many types of real estate without the headache of managing the real estate properties.

A REIT enables small investors to make investments in professionally managed, large, institutional-quality, commercial real estate.

Real Estate can include the following types:

- Office buildings
- Apartments
- Retail stores and shopping malls
- Medical office buildings
- Healthcare facilities
- Rehab properties
- Housing development

Locations of the real estate can be in different areas of the United States.

REIT's have to pay dividends to investors of at least 90% of its taxable income each year. REITs avoid the federal "double taxation" treatment of income that generally results from investments in a corporation.

By diversifying your investment portfolio of stocks, bonds, and cash; REITs provide a decreased risk tolerance and increased return.

The minimum investment in a REIT is not what you might expect if you're thinking it is a high amount. The minimum can be as low as $2500 or $5000. Dividends can start within a few months of your investment and can last for up to 5-8 years, depending on when you invested. REIT's are not liquid investments, but in some cases an investor can sell their shares.

Exchange-traded funds (ETFs):

ETFs started back in the early 90s, so they are considered the new kids on the block. They trade like stocks and they are not actively managed.

Perhaps the best way to explain ETFs is to compare them with Mutual Funds, because an ETF is like an improved mutual fund. One of the major differences is that Mutual Funds are sold or bought at the end of the day after hours, and ETFs are done at the same time they are sold or bought.

It's almost like buying a stock, or selling a stock.

The other major difference is that ETFs expense charges are about half as much as mutual funds. ETFs are defined as index-based investment funds that trade like stocks. ETFs hold assets such as stocks or bonds and seek to trade at approximately the same price as the net asset value of their underlying assets.

Mutual Funds on the other hand are actively managed, versus most ETF's are passively managed. Actively managed mutual funds can eliminate poor performing funds and can make a higher return. Another major advantage that mutual funds have over ETFs is their dominance of retirement assets through their sponsors of MF's. Since mutual funds have been around for a long time (1930's) it is the only investment option in almost all 401k plans in the USA.

To summarize, ETFs have the following advantages over MFs:

Diversification – Since most ETFs track indexes that are made up of a basket of securities, they can provide instant diversification to their shareholders.

Real-time pricing and liquidity – ETFs are bought and sold like stocks, whenever the transaction transpires, and not at the end of day like MF's

Transparency – ETFs are required to disclose their holdings on a daily basis, so you always know exactly what you own.

Lower expense ratios – Most ETFs, which are passive investments, carry expense ratios that are generally lower than those of many actively-managed mutual funds

Tax advantages – ETFs allow investors to pay most of their capital gains upon final sale of the ETF, thereby delaying the tax consequences of owning the position until termination. By contrast, mutual funds generally distribute capital gains to their investors, but ETFs do not.

Today, there are over 1,000 different ETFs that the average investor can purchase, and their choices are just as many as the mutual funds options. From Large-Cap ETFs to International South America ETFs..... from Government bonds to high-yield bonds.....from commodities to real estate..... from technology to precious metals..... there is an ETF for you.

Alternative Investments:

The final type of investment option that is becoming very popular today in America is 'Alternative Investments'. What is an alternative investment? Since stocks and bonds are considered traditional basic investments, like steak & potatoes, alternative investments have a lower correlation than traditional asset classes.

Alternative Investments are complex investments with limited regulation and very un-liquid. For those reasons, ownership of alternative investments is mostly by financial institutions and accredited high-net worth individuals.

Alternative Investments include:

- Hedge funds
- Managed futures
- Real estate
- Commodities and derivatives contracts,
- Precious metals
- Oil & Gas
- And more

If you are in a position to invest in Alternative Investments, the main concern is liquidity. If you put away some of your investment dollars and don't need them or want them for 5-8 years, then you understand Alternative Investments.

While we did not cover every savings program or every investment option available to Americans, we did cover what most people invest in. Financial Institutions do buy and invest in other instruments that are not available to the average person.

We did not discuss the tax ramifications of any of the earnings, gains, of any of the investments.

We will discuss Tax-Plan programs in the next chapter. The tax-plans programs contain all of the investments that we just covered. The taxing of the same investments inside of a tax-plan, and outside of a tax-plan, are both different, which makes tax-plan programs a separate investment option for all of us.

CHAPTER NINE

My Own Money Tax Plans

What would your net worth be today if all the income taxes that you paid to the IRS had been invested for you instead?

Sounds like a dream come true, doesn't it? However, I am sorry to tell you that here in America, we have to pay taxes. But how much tax should you have to pay?

Will Rogers said, *"I am very willing to pay my taxes to my country, but I would be very happy to pay half of my taxes."* I don't know about you, but I would be very proud to be an American and pay half of my taxes, too!

It is up to you to pay less tax. You must work at it and listen to your master mind team of advisors. For the most part, we are concerned with the Federal Income Tax that is withheld from your paychecks. Then if that's not enough, you have to pay the balance when you file your 1040 tax return.

It seems funny that the only required form of financial management or planning is to file a 1040 tax return every year in order to pay taxes to Uncle Sam. The IRS & the government have had 100 years to perfect their system of collecting taxes. That is why they don't count on the individual taxpayer to pay all the taxes they owe with their tax return. No sir, they make the employers do it for them so that it is automatic and mandatory.

Wouldn't it be grand if Uncle Sam made you save and invest money on every paycheck you earn? That would guarantee that you built a nest egg for the future. Basically, the government does make you save at least part of your paycheck, through the FICA deduction. Social Security is where your FICA contribution goes, and your employer matches it. Not a bad deal, when all is said and done.

And while Social Security has its drawbacks and problems, it is no different than the average private citizen when it comes to saving and investing money. When the Social Security Act was created in 1935, it was based on the life expectancy of people. Great Britain had their own 'social security' pension system, and had set age 65 as normal retirement. The United States set age 65 as their normal social security retirement age.

Since that time, there have been several amendments and additions to the Social Security Act, including changing the normal retirement age. Social Security added an annual 'COLA' in 1975, which is a Cost of Living Adjustment. This made Social Security a good pension plan, as long as it is funded, that is.

The social security pension will always have the same problems as any private retirement plan. Changes will be required, starting with more contributions. For the private plan, it's up to the individual to fund it. For Social Security, this means both employers and employees will have to increase the tax paid, through the FICA withdrawn from your paychecks.

Just as your private retirement plan, such as the IRA-401k-SEP, there are three other ways to make sure that Social Security will be available when you retire and when your kids retire.

1. *The earnings or investment returns*

2. *Increase the age for normal retirement*

3. *Lower the formula to equal a lower SS check*

The Social Security problem of the future could be settled today by increasing the contributions of both employers & employees. The problem with this plan is that it is considered an increase in the FICA tax, and who wants to pay more tax?

Why not offset the contributions of both employer & employee with tax credits on their own contributions? One problem would be solved, and the governments need for those tax dollars would have to be met through some other means.

Okay that's enough on Social Security for the moment, we could write another book on it. Keep in mind that social security is a start for each family toward a retirement income.

This chapter focuses on investment and savings programs that will save you federal income taxes, either now, or in the future. The IRS, believe it or not, will be your partner on these programs and not your enemy.

Take advantage of all the tax breaks, deductions and credits you can afford. Use the IRS to leverage additional tax savings for investments.

The first category of Tax-Plans are called tax-deferred and tax-deduction programs.

Tax-Deferred Programs: The majority of the tax plan programs will be under the Tax-Deferred Programs. These are the programs that you will probably recognize. Many of the Retirement Plans are in this category.

Qualified Tax-Plans: These are called qualified because the Internal Revenue Service Code Section and The ERISA Act of 1974 have approved them to be eligible for favored tax treatment. This means tax deductions for each contribution is not taxed, nor the earnings.

When you contribute to a tax plan program like a 401k, 403b, or IRA or a SEP-IRA; you do not pay tax on the contributions. It becomes a tax deduction on your 1040 or business tax-return. That means when you contribute $100, and you save $20 in income taxes, you have effectively made the IRS your partner. You contribute $80 and the IRS $20, but your account now has $100.

In addition, the earnings that your $100 will make is not taxed either, which means that you are getting a double tax benefit from Uncle Sam.

This is a great way to leverage your savings dollars!

If you contribute $5000 over four years, and your employer contributes 50% or $2500, and the earnings made in those four years will equal $7950. Your contribution saved you about $1000 in taxes. So, you end up with a balance of $7950 in your retirement plan, but it only cost you $4000 in after-tax contributions. Pretty good leverage, don't you think?

There are many more tax plans that qualify for this type of savings/investment program. They just have different IRS names, such as:

- Pension Plans
- Profit-Sharing Plans
- 457 Plans
- Simple Plans
- And More

These plans are different, but all have the same benefits.

In discussing these tax plans, there is no mention of what type of investment or savings accounts to use. As we said earlier, you need to be focused on the tax considerations of accumulating wealth or net worth.

When will you pay taxes on these programs? Most programs are set up so that you will pay the taxes when you start taking out the income. This usually occurs in your retirement years. The major goal of these programs is to provide income to you when you are not working. If you are getting less income in retirement, then you should be paying less tax because you are now in a lower tax bracket.

This is why these programs are popular with most people. You get a tax break on your contribution, it grows tax-deferred, and when you take out the income---you pay less tax. Sounds good, but that also means you will be making less income than when you were working.

Who wants that? Do you? Will you be able to enjoy the retirement you're looking forward to in your Golden Years if you have to live on a shoestring?

Let's move into the second type of Tax Plan.

Non-Qualified Tax Plans: The major difference on these tax-plans is that the contribution or your savings is not deductible or tax favored. However, the earnings of these programs is just like the qualified plans, being tax deferred until you take the income out of it. There are several non-qualified plans available.

Tax favored annuities and max-funded life insurance programs are the two types that many Americans invest in each year. If you think in terms of non-qualified, it simply means that there are really no limits on the contributions since there is no tax deduction. This can be a good investment strategy for building net worth and your financial goals.

The third category of taxation is not technically called non-qualified, but not exactly qualified plans, either. We will call these C3, for Category 3.

The best way to understand the taxation of each investment.... whether it is now, in the future, or never....is to describe each of the Tax-Plans by its name. You may or may not be familiar with these plans.

QP—Qualified Plans:

IRA-Individual Retirement Plans: This is also called a Traditional IRA, for saving and investing for retirement on a tax-deferred basis and a tax-deductible basis. This is excellent if you do not have a current qualified retirement plan through your employer. If you have a qualified retirement plan at work, depending on your income, can you qualify for a tax deduction? One of this plan's best options is that a non-working spouse qualifies for an IRA.

In addition, there are maximum contributions and a catch-up provision for people age 50 and older to fund their IRA. Check online for the current year maximum and catch-up amounts. There is a 10% penalty if you make a withdrawal from your IRA before you are age 59.5. You must take an RMD, or required minimum distribution, by age 70.5.

Employer-401K: This retirement plan is sponsored by the Employer and is considered the 'big' retirement plan. Both the employer and the employee can contribute to this plan. Many large companies have a 401k and will make a contribution that is about a 6% match, provided the employee contributes 6%. Some employers will match half of an employee's contribution, up to a certain maximum amount. The employee can increase their contribution over the matching plan, and there is also a catch-up age 50 & over provision to contribute more. The 401k contribution can be four to five times the IRA contribution.

There is usually a loan option that, by itself, is a 'special benefit' for the employee, although it is a huge administrative expense for the employer. This benefit saves employees a lot of taxes, because when they borrow from their 'own' 401k, there is no taxable event.

If there was an option to withdraw money from a 401k, it would be taxable that same year and a 10% penalty would be added. If the employee were to leave their employer, for whatever reason, they have several options for their 401k.

First, if they just take the money, the employer will withhold 20% of their total 401k, and the employee will have to pay taxes on a 100% of their account. In addition, if the employee is under the age of 59 and a half, they will pay a 10% penalty. The second option is to rollover the 401k retirement plan to a new employer's retirement plan, which could be a 401k too. And the third option is to do a Rollover to their IRA, whether it is a new IRA or existing one. On the two rollover options, there are no taxes or penalties to pay. IRS views it as you moving money from one IRA to another IRA, so it's the same.

The major difference in moving a 401k (retirement plan) to the employer's plan or their own IRA is that, with an IRA, you have many more options on what investments you want to use.

When you retire and leave your employer, you can also do a Rollover (transfer) to an IRA account, whether it is an existing IRA plan or a new one.

The major reason that the IRS and Congress created the Retirement Plans was so that everyone would save money for their retirement years. It takes a godly amount of money in your retirement plan to be able to draw income from it for the rest of your life. How much money you have at your disposal depends on the goals you set for retirement.

To know how much you may need in your retirement plan, let's see what your income is worth. If you are making $50,000 a year now, we will assume that's what you need for retirement. It will take a retirement asset of $1,250,000 paying 4% conservatively to equal $50,000 a year and not reduce the principle.

But there lies the major obstacle in retirement planning.

How much will you need five years after retirement, or ten years, or after 20 years? When you are working, your income tends to rise with employment raises and cost of living adjustments. When you retire, any raises have to come from your retirement assets and Social Security income. Most people will need more than the $1.2 million to pay for inflation and maintain their standard of living

Indi-401k: The individual 401k is only for the small business owners with no employees other than their spouse. At the same time, though, it allows for higher limits of contributions such as the big 401k-Employer plan. And that includes the Simplified Employer Plan (SEP). This plan is perfect for the Home-Based business or an Internet business in which one spouse or both run the business.

SEP-IRA: This is for the business owner and his employees. The owner can contribute, or match, a similar amount contribution, as a 401k allows. The SEP law says that whatever percentage is contributed for the owner, the same percentage applies to their employees. This can be a blessing or a big expense item for the owner of the small business.

SIMPLE: This is another small business type of retirement plan that is far more generous for the employer's contribution to their employees. In other words, the employer can contribute less than the SEP plan and still be able to contribute a nice amount for the owner's part.

The one common denominator on all qualified retirement plans is that there cannot be any discrimination. And it is not because of the employee's skin color or race, but on their status as an employee. For example, if all employees work 30 hours or more a week and have been working for six months, they have to be included in the company's retirement plan

403: These qualified plans are like 401ks in the private sector, but are for Education Organizations such as public schools, and non-profits. Some 403b's have a matching contribution from their employer. That being said, many 403b plans, especially in the public school system, have no employer contribution and are optional retirement plans.

457: This is similar to a 403b plan for non-profits and educational organizations. The contribution amounts for both the 403b and the 457 plans are the same maximums as the 401k plans.

PROFIT-SHARING PLAN (PSP): many private companies use a PSP in addition to their regular retirement plan (401k) for extra incentive to their employees. If the company has a profit, then a portion of that profit will go to each employee PSP. There are also companies that only have a PSP because they cannot set up a regular retirement plan, probably because they don't feel they can afford it. This way, when the company makes a profit and they have the monies, they can contribute to the PSP.

PENSION: The Pension Plan used to be the dominant type of retirement plan in the USA for many years. This is the plan where your retirement income is based on your years of service, your annual salary, and a formula to pay the retiree a monthly income check for life.

ROTH-IRA: This is one of the newest retirement plans, and even though considered a qualified plan, there is no tax deduction on the contribution to the ROTH-IRA or ROTH-401k. The opposite happens on withdrawal for retirement income---it is tax-free. Yes, tax-free, no taxes to be paid. Many people prefer to get the tax-break now than wait until later.

The ROTH is increasing in contributions every year. Many employees that have maxed out their traditional 401k or IRA can also contribute to the ROTH, depending on their income. Also, remember that if your tax-bracket is higher in retirement---the opposite of what everybody says--- then the ROTH or tax-free programs can net you more income.

ROTH-401K: This is becoming almost mandatory in 401k plans, especially with the larger American Companies. The employee can choose between their traditional 401k, before tax, and the ROTH contribution, after tax, or a combination of both.

NQ—Non-Qualified: The following is an added definition and the benefits of 'Qualified Plans' which, if not included, will make the plan a Non-Qualified Plan.

The main difference, as we said earlier, is that a QP has better tax treatment because the employer and the employee or business owner can deduct their contribution, then the earnings of the plan are tax-deferred.

A Non-Qualified Plan has no preferred tax-treatment on any of the contributions and it also does not have:

- Disclosure of all the documents
- Coverage of a specific percentage of employees
- Participation of eligible employees is required.
- No discrimination of lower paid employees
- Employees are vested in the plan after some years

There are really two types of Non-Qualified Plans, and these two types of products are in more American households than the total number of Qualified plans. Plus, these two types of plans are marketed by every insurance company in the USA.

ANNUITIES: This is the first non-qualified plan. These investment products allow unlimited contribution on an after tax basis, but the earnings are tax-deferred until the income is taken out. What makes the earnings inside of the annuity?

Good question!

The answer is: Everything!

Securities such as mutual funds made up of stocks & bonds, cash, and fixed accounts from the general fund of life insurance companies.

When it is time to withdraw income from these accounts, there are several options. The first option is simply to cash it in, and then in turn you receive your principle back, plus the earnings. The earnings are taxable as ordinary income. Your second option is to take out monthly or annual income checks. Annuities always pay out the earnings first. This means that you will have to pay taxes on all you receive for some years, and when the principle is withdrawn, you will pay no taxes.

The third option for many people may be the reason they contributed to an annuity in the first place. They can now turn that annuity into an annuitized stream on income payments for life. In addition, each income payment is calculated as part principle & part earnings, to spread the taxable part over a lifetime.

Annuities are also creditor proof in most of the states, just the same as Qualified Plans. This means that a creditor cannot sue for the annuity because it is considered a retirement plan.

LIFE INSURANCE: Life Insurance has been around for hundreds of years. It was initially designed for, and still does, replace the lost wages of the breadwinner or winners of a family. But it is used for countless other financial goals or problems. Believe it or not, it has evolved into one of the top tax-free investment plans in the United States.

Remember, we are now in the Tax-Plans section and have already mentioned back in the Asset protection section how life insurance protects the biggest asset a family has---the father, mother, husband and wife. In addition, it provides protection to pay off all mortgage payments and any outstanding debts. It can be used to pay Estate Taxes if your estate is big enough, and that is what we all want, right?

Life Plans are used by business owners, Corporations, Public Companies and Trusts to insure the key individuals, managers, trustees, CEO's and VP's from losses if something happened to one or more of them. Business partners & shareholders use Life Insurance Plans to value their Corporation or Business, so that if someone dies the life plan will pay for their equity participation.

Today the Life Plans continue to provide the benefits of yesterday and much, much more. The first benefit is that life insurance costs are considerably less today than a few years ago. If you recall, our mortality rates here in the US are lower because Americans are living longer, a lot longer.

The new benefits of today also include additions to a permanent Life policy, which are called riders and packaged with the plan. These include ABR-accelerated benefit riders, unheard of a few years ago. These riders will pay benefits to the client or policy owner while the person is alive. This would include benefits for a terminal illness months before death, and allow withdrawal of some of the insurance monies for whatever the policyholder wants to do.

There is also a critical illness benefit that pays a certain amount to the client for a major heart attack, cancer, stroke and more. Finally, there is a 'chronic' type benefit that pays for 'long-term care' expenses.

The Tax-Free benefit for taking a withdrawal or a lifetime of income checks is still new to the American public. The major reason is that when most people hear the term "life insurance," they may start running in fear that they're about to be barraged with hard sell tactics.

This anxiety is understandable because of the vast numbers of insurance agents, many whose careers didn't last long. But, this is also changing and today there are less insurance agents in the market. There may come a time when the client, or policy owner, will call for a professional insurance agent. In fact many people in the United States today have no insurance professional, or have never visited with one.

The 'Technical and Miscellaneous Revenue Act of 1988' made the permanent life insurance programs an extraordinary plan for tax-free income. The law limits the maximum amount of contributions for funding a life insurance plan. But what is not known to the average citizen is that the maximum consists of quite a lot of money that may be contributed. By investing in a tax-free Life-Plan, a person can receive tax-free benefits for life if they so choose.

Now that you know where the tax-free came from, let's analyze the components of an individual program. As you may recall, this is a non-qualified plan, which means the contribution amounts are not deductible from your taxable income. On the other end, when it is taken out to spend or for retirement living, it is tax-free. This is almost the opposite of the 'Qualified Plans'.

How important or how strong is a tax-free plan?

If you were to take out income from a qualified plan such as an IRA and you were in your 60s, then you would pay taxes on that amount. If you took income from a Life-Plan, it would be tax-free.

Let's compare:

Let's say that you take out $10,000 in one year and you are officially in the 28% tax bracket. If it came from your IRA, you would pay about $2,800 in taxes, and take home $7200. On the tax-free plan, if you take out $10,000, then you net the same $10,000. Another way of doing this is to take out only $7200 net, and let the other $2800 continue to grow.

This is the power of tax-free income. But, there is another major reason to consider a tax-free type of a life plan.

We know that the ROTH plans are tax-free, and we will cover municipal bonds which is also a tax-free plan. If you have a diversified investment portfolio to make sure you don't have all your eggs in one basket, shouldn't you also beware of having all your 'tax-eggs' in one basket?

As discussed earlier, most of us have the majority of our assets or monies in Qualified Tax Plans, like 401(k)'s & IRA's. This means that even if you have more retirement assets in retirement, you will have to pay the Federal Income Tax based on whatever tax bracket you are in. That can be good or bad.

Let us assume that you will not be in a lower tax-bracket in retirement, but a higher one because that is what you wanted. It was a financial goal to accumulate more assets. Why else are you reading this book, right?

What this means to you is that if Federal Income Taxes increase over the years, and even if you are in a lower tax bracket, you could pay a lot of tax. That is why a diversification of tax plans is very good for planning your total portfolio.

The biggest fear that can happen is that the IRS and Congress make changes on the current Tax Laws. They could change the RMD-required minimum distribution age to a earlier age. They can take away exemptions and they can increase the tax rates, and even stop the tax deductions.

Get with your Advisor team to go over your investment diversification and your tax plan diversification.

C3: Category Three is about the rest of the types of taxation that can fall on your investments. These include:

- Capital gains tax
- Non-taxable earnings
- Some overlapping of the NQP tax strategies

It sounds a little weird, doesn't it? But not to worry---the IRS knows how to calculate it and tax it.

MUNICIPAL BONDS: Similar to regular bonds, which means that MB are 'debt instruments' issued by governmental entities such as cities, counties and states. Since these government entities have to pay the investors, their cost of that capital is a lower interest rate than the private bonds pay out. But the interest to the investor is 'tax-free 'or 'tax-exempt'.

When a person invests in municipal bonds, they are investing in debt instruments. We have covered what debt instruments are and how they are affected in the market and what their earnings are. Sometimes the tax-exempt return of a Municipal Bond is higher than the after tax-return of a taxable bond. And the opposite is also true. But both types of bonds have similar risks.

The other part of the Municipal Bonds tax question is that when the bonds are sold and a profit is made, they are subject to capital-gains taxation. Bond prices & market value are higher when interest rates are lower.

MUTUAL FUNDS: These are taxed both ways. They are taxed as ordinary income when they pay short-term dividends, and they are subject to capital gains for long-term dividends and profit on their sale.

REIT: Real Estate Investment Trusts are also taxed both ways. The income from the trust is subject to ordinary income tax and the profit from the sale is a capital gain.

Capital-Gains treatment of taxation is not as good as tax-free, but definitely much better than ordinary taxation. Ordinary Tax means that 100% of your earnings or profits are subject to your tax-bracket for payment of income taxes. Capital Gains tax treatment means that the profit that is made on the sale of the investment asset.

Capital Gains Tax rates can increase just like ordinary tax rates increase. And since we are on the subject of tax-rates, Corporate Tax rates can change also.

So you have ordinary tax-rates, capital-gains tax rates, corporate tax rates, tax-deferred and tax free that will be applied to your assets. Now you know why you should have a master-mind advisor group to save you thousands and thousands of dollars---maybe million of dollars---in taxes that could be part of your net worth.

ALTERNATIVE: Alternative investments can have all of what we have shown for taxation. Ordinary tax for dividends, capital gains for profits of sale, and they might also have some good tax-deductions too. The tax deductions will mean that the IRS will become your partner and save Income Taxes. This means part of the investment is funded by tax dollars. And the tax-deduction amount can be a large one.

The other part of this is that on some Alternative Investments, there is a depletion tax credit for part of the income or dividend. In other words, if you have a 15% depletion credit, then only 85% of your income or dividend would be subject to taxation.

If you are building a net worth, then every tax dollar you can save means more dollars for your investments, which means more assets, and finally a higher net worth. The Federal Income Tax laws can change at any time. Planning for the year and future years can be a big difference in the taxes you pay.

As a free American, you always have a choice: you can contribute more to the IRS, or the IRS can contribute more to you.

CHAPTER TEN

My Own Real Estate Investments

When you start talking about investing in Real Estate, you need to find out the historical return of real estate after inflation, for any time period. Next, you should compare it to stocks as far as a return. After all, both investments are 'ownership' types of investments.

There are many investors that are pro-real estate, and then there are the pro-stock investors. Because of this, they tend to do more research on what stocks to invest in and/or what real estate to buy.

While a small percentage of investors can buy stocks on margin, or a loan, and leverage to a higher return....most don't. Not, that is, as compared to real estate, which is leveraged all the time through financing the property. Real Estate investing is the same as getting financing. Usually, you can't or won't do one without the other.

When you buy real estate, you are either going to live on the real estate, or you will sell the property at a future date. The amount of your mortgage payment is similar to renting an apartment. So, why would you even consider paying for the house in cash? The odds are that you will sell that house in the future.

When you are considering investing in real estate for a return on investment, the greater return on investment is usually a leverage financed deal.

If you invest in real estate that will provide rental income, whether it be a duplex, eight-plex, or an apartment building; the rent pays for the loan and hopefully all other expenses as well. Then, one day in the future, the owner sells the property and makes a capital-gain profit---which is at least half the tax of ordinary tax rates.

This is why investors purchase real estate.

Real Estate-Raw Land: The least type of investment purchased by the average investor is in raw land. There are two major obstacles that hold back the average investor.

1. *There is no rental income to support the cost of the capital to invest in raw land.*
2. *You must prepare to live off your other income sources and won't count on selling the property for a while.*

If you invest in all the other real estate types and get experience over the years, you can consider raw land as an investment return. There have been many highly excited, emotion driven, speculative investors that just "know" their raw land purchase will sell for a 100 times its cost in two to five years. Then to their sorrow, after 20 years there hasn't even been an offer.

Be very careful when considering raw land!

Real Estate-Rental Properties: When investing in rental properties, you are actually buying a rental unit. Most of the time, the price is high market value where rental property is in demand. The seller knows how much income the rental unit brings in, and that income can create the sales price.

If you want to finance the investment real estate rental property, most lenders will want at least 20% from the investor and finance the 80%. For the first time real estate investor, the down payment of 20% can be a major obstacle. You will have to get the cash from your liquid investments, without hurting your emergency reserves or incurring any penalties or extra fees to get the money.

When you are buying your second or third property, the leverage of your first rental property and also a lower down payment, or portion of the loan you must finance, can make getting the money much easier.

This is why many people get into trouble and end up with a foreclosure if they did buy the property or are not able to purchase the real estate at all. The fixed mindset wants to buy real estate. The fixed mindset says you can be a real estate mogul. But in the end your fixed mindset was wrong. It didn't know any better.

Rental real estate can offer you two types of investment return, and that is why many owners will keep their rental investment for a while. We will say it again: rental income can pay all the expenses and make a profit, so that you can sell it in the future for another profit (capital-gain profit).

The other item you should consider when investing in rental real estate, or in 'flipping' real estate, is the amount of time & expense to do whatever repairs or renovations are needed. This can be a major expense and be the difference between making a profit or a loss. You have to buy at a decent price and the rental unit needs to be marketable without investing a major sum in renovating it.

Real Estate Flipping: You might say that the opposite of rental real estate is 'flipping' real estate. However, it doesn't have to be. Flipping means that you want to purchase a property at below market value, fix it up and then sell it at market value or higher in a short time period. Ideally, you can resell in 3-6 months.

If improvements are necessary, due to a slow real estate market, you might not want to buy a property. But, with some investors whose primary focus is flipping, there may be a plan B in case the property can't be sold right away. You might rent it for a while, until the market for real estate improves.

You can be a real estate investor and invest in both types of properties, both rental & flipping. If you can get a good rental income, you may not wish to sell or flip, either, for a while. And if the property you invested in was for rental purposes, but your realtor advisor says that you can sell it quickly for a great return, then by all means, do it!

Some investors that have been buying and selling real estate for a while have gotten so good at it they can buy it one day and sell it the next. When this happens, the investor will have to schedule two closings:

1. *One to buy it*
2. *One to sell it*

This is a good profit situation!

If you do buy real estate and then sell it in less than a year, you will have a short-term capital gain, which means it is all taxable. Don't be alarmed, because a profit is a profit. If you made $100 in interest or dividends, you would pay ordinary tax, too. If you sell the real estate after a year, it is a long-term capital gain and your tax will be considerably less.

Another way to make a good profit or income is to sell the property at a certain price, even a higher than market value price, because you are financing all or part of the sale. Besides getting a higher selling price, you will get interest on the mortgage which is always a higher interest rate.

You have to do some extra work in this type of arrangement, because you will have to draw up the contract, the mortgage note, and the terms of the agreement. The buyer will honor your terms and make all the payments. For many, this is the only way they are able to buy a home of their own.

Real Estate Commercial: Investing in commercial real estate is not something for the average investor. And most real estate investors will never buy any commercial real estate, nor do they want to, even if they could. The major reason is that the pricing or market value is higher than other real estate.

But, what if you could come up with the money to buy a nice size commercial piece of property, then what? Should you do it?

Basically, you will have two options: Either you have to turn it into an income rental property, or you have to sell it. If the commercial property is a fixer-upper and you have to spend a lot of money to make it marketable, think long and hard about buying it. The selling process could take a long time. Can you afford to make payments on the property without any rental income, or no sale for more than a year or two?

A good commercial investor will also have experience in finding the right type of tenant for rental properties. You must learn to be choosy and not accept any tenant you feel will be harmful in attracting the wrong type of customers to the commercial site.

Anyway, if you have an interest in commercial investing; take your time and learn more than you know now. Get into the 'growth' mindset and have an exit strategy that will not hurt your other investments and savings accounts.

Real Estate Investment Trusts (REITS): What are REITS? Have you heard this real estate term before? We discussed REITS in both the tax-plans and the stock market chapters. Now, we'll discuss REITS in the real estate section of this book.

REITS could be part or all of the commercial real estate you want to own. You can invest in REITS without the added risks and liabilities of commercial real estate.

The definition of a REIT is the following:

'Any corporation, trust or association that acts as an investment agent specializing in real estate and real estate mortgages. REITs are required to distribute at least 90% of their taxable income into the hands of investors. A REIT is a company that owns, and in most cases, operates income-producing real estate. REITs own many types of commercial real estate, ranging from office and apartment buildings to warehouses, hospitals, shopping centers, hotels and even real estate in New York City.'

The REIT structure was designed to provide a real estate investment structure similar to the structure mutual funds provides for investment in stocks. An investment of money into a REIT is an investment in several-multiple real estate properties.

So, like a mutual fund holds many different stocks, a REIT can hold many different real estate properties. The real estate is usually scattered all over the United States to decrease and spread the risk even further.

When we discussed commercial real estate, we did not mention any exact pricing or purchase prices of any property. We mentioned that a person could invest in a REIT without the traditional risks and liabilities of commercial real estate.

Now, we can actually mention REIT pricing for investing. Are you ready for this? How about $5000 or $10,000, or even $25,000? Plus, on top of that, you don't have to be involved in the maintenance or the services that real estate tenants demand.

Almost all REITS require that the investor have a certain annual income and net worth to qualify for a REIT purchase. This is one way that the industry can help the potential investor in understanding that this type of investment is not liquid. But, you understand that if you owned a commercial piece of property, it is not particularly liquid, either.

Real Estate Investment-Home: The final Real Estate Property is your own personal residence. You are probably thinking that the home should have been covered first, because the home is the first real estate property that Americans own.

The truth is that most people have a fixed mindset on investing in, or purchasing, a home or homes in their lifetime. How many homes do you think the average person buys in their lifetime? The answer is three. Their first home is their 'beginner' home versus renting an apartment and kissing that money goodbye. The second bigger home they buy because they have kids and need more space. Finally, the third home is the retirement and last home.

Is there anything that says you can't purchase seven to ten homes in your lifetime? At this point, you might be wondering why on earth you'd want to move that often, as it's a giant pain in the asset.

But, what if you made a good profit on every move or every sale of your former home? What if it was fun to plan a move and a new investment purchase of a home? What if it was an enjoyable game? Different mindset?

Currently, the tax laws of the USA state that a family, joint-filers, can exempt up to $500,000 in gains on the sale of their personal residence. That means no taxes---just money to invest in and save.

The IRS tax law also says that the couple-family has to live in the house for two years, and have owned the house for two years before the sale. This means that if it was necessary to rent your home for any reason, as long as you owned it and lived in it for two years of the five years prior to the sale, you qualify for the exemption.

Now the exciting part---you can get the exemption of up to $500k for each and every home that you sell!

There is NO limit! Will you make $500k on every home you have lived in and sell it? Maybe not, but, it doesn't matter; you can still make a tax-exempt profit and sock it away.

The best way to show you how to maximize the profit on the sale of a home and receive the tax-exempt profit is through a PLAN. Yes..... planning to buy and sell ten homes in your lifetime. It doesn't matter if you don't sell all ten, because this PLAN has a built in a conservative exit strategy.

You will have to factor in your ages, the years that you plan to buy & sell your homes, the market values of your area and the estimated profit. This will take some time, but it will be well worth it and you can build your net worth.

THE-TAX-FREE-BUY-MY-HOMES-PLAN:

- You purchase a home at a MV price
- You sell the house in 2-5 years
- Take the Profit and invest it
- Buy your 2nd home
- Sell it in 2-5 years.
- Take the tax-exemption profit and invest it.
- Buy your 3rd -10th Home???

It's a simple plan. The hard part will be your planning, and it will consist of the areas that you want to move to. Will these be within your state or out of state? Will you have to move sooner because of a career change? Will the real estate market get you the highest profit on every sale?

It will take some work and good planning. So, make it a game and have some fun with it. Just imagine that it is an adventure to look for a new home every two to five years. You can make it a goal to live in different types of home architecture, and live in different counties, cities, states, or on the river's edge, or by the ocean, or in the mountains, etc.

Now for the conservative strategies, just in case everything doesn't go the way you want it to if you want to make a profit.

The Real Estate Market will always change and there will be times when you can sell at a higher market value, or a lower market value. There can be times that the market might be out of your control. This can happen when you are changing jobs, or transferring to another work location. But it doesn't matter, because having this plan will not hurt you.

The worst that can happen is this---if you want to sell your house today and won't be able to make a good profit, or would even take a loss....don't sell yet. You can always stay in the house until things look better.

Of course if you have no job or income, then you are not in the same plan anymore. This could happen if you were living in your first home or your 5th home, correct?

If you have to sell a home because a new job and you haven't lived it in for two years, or if you sold it today and you took a loss, those events had nothing to do with your plan because they would have happened anyway.

A written Plan on making a tax-exempt profit is a worthwhile goal or hobby. A family could put away $100,000, or even a million, in tax-exempt profits. It depends on your income and your future income, because income will determine how much of home you can purchase.

Real Estate will always be there, and as they say....there is only so much real estate in the world, we can't make anymore. So, it will always be valuable and its value will only grow with time.

CHAPTER ELEVEN

My Own Business Equity

A business of your own may be necessary for you to reach the financial net worth you have in mind. It doesn't mean that you have to start a business. It only means that you may not reach your goals through the other three accumulation vehicles.

The major difference in creating business equity as a source of wealth, versus the other three types, is that the business requires more active involvement. You already know that investing in Real Estate, Tax-Plans, and The Stock Market are more passive investing than active.

It is not that you could be become very active in investing in the three, but most people do not have to or even want to. On the other hand, you really don't have that choice when you own a business. You need to be active in the business.

But, a business can make more money than the three other investment types. All public corporations are businesses, really big businesses. At one time, though, their public corporation might have been as big as a 'lemonade stand' in front of their house.

How did any small business grow to become a big business and a public corporation? How did the business go from selling 3 units a day to 1000 units a day? On the day the business went public, the business owner became wealthy or wealthier. Overnight, they were worth millions.

The major reason, if not the only reason, that the small business went public was that the business developed a system that was on automatic, producing sales every day.

The business owner made many decisions over the life of the business to change it, so that it became an automatic business system. This is how 'business equity' is created. It is a real asset that has market value.

When a business goes public, it means that the business will have access to all the financing or money it needs in order to grow. If you remember from the 'market' chapter, we said that Public Corporations were the only entities that could issue bonds or debt instruments, stocks or equities. From this side of the coin, the public company can get money from 'borrowing money' through the bond issues, and can sell stock shares to also raise money.

How each public corporation uses the money to make money is up to its board, its advisory team and its stockholders. The more sales the company can make, the more profit. The more profit, the more dividends are paid. This drives up the stock price, or the equity worth of each stock share.

Many of the products and services that we Americans use every day were started by a small business that eventually became a public corporation. ATT-Corp., Proctor & Gamble, McDonalds, Microsoft, and Apple, to name just a few.

Anyone in America can build a business that can become a public corporation. That is our right and our freedom. We live in the greatest Capitalistic, Free-Enterprise System in the world. But we also have the right to build a business at home and make a million dollars a year too.

The Public Company is like the final goal for business success.... the ultimate destination....what we all want if we could do it....the impossible dream. But, in today's business environment, you don't have to. Who knows? Tomorrow, or in a few years; your growth mindset may tell you that now is the time to build a public company or conversely, that you never have to.

Just in case you don't, let's list the other 99% of ways to do business, build equity and make money.

The first 'fixed mindset' on getting into business is to NOT do what the majority of business owners do. They set up a business to work for themselves. Isn't that what you would do if you started a business?

That question is one of those with a yes and a no answer.

Most businesses, including all small & home businesses too, only make income through sales. That's it. They do not make a dime when they retire the business, or quit, or sell parts of the business assets. They do not have to go public to make a profit on the 'equity' value of the business. But they do need the business to have a 'value' to sell.

If you go into business just to quit your job and not have a boss anymore, that's not a good reason. It can be a good reason for you to 'Plan' a business venture. You don't want to go from working for a bad boss to working for another boss that is even worse---yourself.

Can you make a lot of money in business just from the sales of a single product or service? Yes, you can. If you do this for a long time, say ten years or so, that means you could have built systems into the business so that one day after making all the money from sales, you double up with the sale of the business.

Would you invest in a rental house and make a good profit every year from the income and then after several years of profit give the rental house to the current tenant? Of course not, but, that is what businesses do every day. They give away their business or just plain let it go. That dratted 'fixed mindset' at work again!

We need to define some of the business terms, just as if you were starting a business today and were new to the business world. In other words, as if you don't know the first thing about business. Here's the beauty of it: you don't have to know anything about it if you follow the rules and proper steps.

What type of organized business entity structure are you going to use to run your business?

Will it be a part-time business or a full-time business? There are several types of business entities and each has its benefits and its own red tape, especially in the beginning.

Many of the more precarious moments can be avoided if you are running at full speed. Remember, you need to use all available resources to help strengthen your mindset if you are serious about building your business and net worth.

You will never be successful if you cut corners, especially if you choose to invest in starting your own business, because your business can end up looking like no more than a project that you do in your spare time.

There is a difference between a part-time business plan and something that you do to just sort of piddle around in your spare time.

What type of entity will you choose? The following shows the different types of business entity choices that are available:

The Sole Proprietorship:

The simplest type of business to run is a sole proprietorship. If you name your business after yourself, using only your first name, last name, or both (e.g., Robert Garcia), and have no employees, you don't have to file an "assume name certificate" or obtain a new employer identification number (EIN) from the IRS. You can use your social security number.

If you use a name that is different from your own name, you will probably have to file an "assume name certificate" in each county where you conduct business. If your business employs persons other than yourself, you will need to obtain an EIN (employer identification number) from the IRS. You will need this number to pay the withholding tax and the FICA contributions made.

For your income tax filing, you will simply file a schedule C with your IRS 1040 income tax return to report your sales, cost of goods sold, and expenses. Then, take your net profit or loss on your IRS 1040 page one, and pay income taxes and self-employment social security taxes on your total business income.

Although this is the easiest type of business entity, all liabilities rest on your shoulders. You and the business entity are now one and the same. Creditors can come after you individually for any debts, obligations, or liabilities of the business. Lawsuits can be filed against you and your business. A sole proprietorship may offer the least amount of tax write-offs and deductions, depending on your net profits.

On the other hand, it is the easiest to set up, and with good recommendations from your advisory board, you can get liability insurance to protect yourself.

The Partnership:

You and your partner can combine twice the resources, including capital and time, to help the business grow twice as fast. A partnership is probably the least used type of business entity being utilized today.

Why? Because one partner may do more work and earn more profits than the other, but each partner is legally responsible for the other's actions. Each partner can be financially responsible for all of the debts, obligations, and liabilities of the partnership.

When a good partnership works it is because each of the partners is doing his or her share of the workload, and each partner has a special expertise that they have implemented for the business.

After that, either the Partnership will be dissolved because one partner or more is not contributing much to the business; or all the partners are doing a great job of working and making money but they still dissolve the partnership for one reason or another. They may set up a Corporation with each partner receiving shares equal to their partnership interest.

The Subchapter S-Corporation:

There are two features enjoyed by subchapter S-corporations that offer great benefits at the start. The first is that the business itself is a separate entity and is not attached to your personal assets and liabilities. This is because the corporation structure allows for limited liability to its shareholders.

Secondly, the subchapter S-corporation tax reporting rules require that all profits or losses reported on its 1120-S tax return pass through the corporate entity to the individual shareholder's personal IRS 1040 income tax return.

The C-Corporation:

The C-Corp. is very unique in many ways. The first way, and it may be new to you, is that for the first time in your life you will have to file two tax returns for the same year.

What?! Read on, and all will be made clear.

The Corporate return is called a 1120 and through this tax return you would report all sales and expenses and profits or losses.

You will also file your own individual IRS 1040 tax return to report any salaries, bonuses, or dividends you receive as the primary or only stockholder of your Corporation. This is where the word 'double-taxation' comes from. Ugh! The C-Corp has its own Federal Income Tax Schedule and must pay corporate taxes based on the tax bracket that it is in.

The business owner or primary working stockholder will pay Corporate Taxes and Personal 1040 income taxes. It doesn't mean that because of this the owner will pay more, it just means that two returns will be filed to pay taxes.

Everything depends on the sales volume of the Corp-C, along with the expenses, inventories, salaries of workers, paid benefits and more. All these things determine the final adjusted gross income.

Benefits for all employees, even if there is just a handful, and for the owners is one reason to form a C-Corp. The benefits are usually tax-deductible benefits that can be used by the owners. This includes medical plans, retirement plans, and special benefits.

Any dividends paid to the stockholders are taxable on their personal IRS 1040 tax return, and of course they will pay taxes on those dividends. The C-Corp has many tax-deductible features not found in other business entities. Other benefits that are available for a C-Corp include:

- Limited Liability to protect personal assets from creditors and lawsuits.

- A medical reimbursement plan that allows the corporation to deduct all payments paid for medical benefits up to a fixed dollar limit. The shareholders, including the owners, receive this benefit tax-free.

- A C-Corp can attract more start-up capital and expansion capital, because there is more flexibility in setting up ownership arrangements.

- If there is a possibility of going public, you must have a C-Corp.
- A C-Corp has the ability to accumulate earnings for future expansion at a lower tax cost than the other entities.

The biggest hurdle or problem you will probably run into for setting up a C-Corp is actually setting it up, plus the required paperwork. You have two choices:

1. *Do it yourself and save on fees but incur a lot of work*
2. *Hire your Advisory team members, the attorney or the tax-professional-CPA to set up the Corporation for you, and pay more fees.*

The Limited Liability Company (LLC):

The limited liability company, or LLC, is a type of business entity that will protect the owners' or members' liability exposure through the limited liability feature. The LLC can choose how it files its tax return: through an IRS form 1040, schedule C, like a sole proprietorship if there is only one member, an IRS form 1065, like a partnership if there is more than one member, or an IRS form 1120 or 1120-S, like a corporation if it files an IRS form 8832 "Choice of Entity" election to be taxed as an association.

You have many choices in establishing your business entity.

Your tax professional and attorney team members can help you set up the right entity for you, as well as make sure that you are fully compliant with state law requirements and IRS standards.

Many owners of good businesses get into trouble with the IRS because they didn't know that they had to pay quarterly income taxes and payroll taxes. Unfortunately, the IRS does not consider ignorance of the law a valid reason for not paying your taxes. When you set up your business entity books correctly from the beginning, your business sales, and therefore your profits, can grow faster. So, it pays to do it right the first time.

Now that you have chosen your business entity, what kind of business are you going to run? There are thousands of business choices.

Will you run a traditional retail business and use a storefront to sell your goods? Or, will you have a franchised business with a turnkey business plan, and pay a royalty fee to the franchise owners?

How about a network marketing business in which you distribute products or services to the consumer at either the wholesale or retail level?

Can you sell your products or services on the Internet?

Types of Businesses that you can set up and own:

- Retail Business
- Wholesale Business
- Manufacturers Business
- Franchise Business
- Direct Sales Business
- Network-Marketing Business
- Distribution Business
- Home-Based Business
- Computer Business

- Internet Business
- Service Only Business
- Consultant Business
- Infopreneur Business

Start doing your homework and research all types of business plans. When you like the industry and the business, then start researching the Companies that may offer a Franchised business plan, and/or the vendors and providers of the products you will need for the business.

The Infopreneur Business Model:

We have mentioned an Infopreneur Business as one of your choices. While we might have covered each of the business types, it is much better for you to research from scratch and learn all you can about the business industry.

The reason we will discuss the 'Infopreneur' business is that it is one of the newer business plans. Plus, you can run the infopreneur business in addition to any other business and the infopreneur business can help you make a healthy profit on your first business.

OMG, you're kidding, right?

Wrong.

Just what is this 'Infopreneur' business, anyway?

The infopreneur business is the business of marketing and selling information. Have you ever thought of being an author and writing a book? How about writing an e-Book on your existing business and selling that book online?

You probably bought this book, 'My Own Financial Blueprint', in order to receive the information on how to build net worth and financial independence. The book contains information and the book was sold, so the author is an infopreneur.

How do you market and sell information? There are many ways to sell information. If you look around you will see that there is a lot of information out there to be found. There is information that no one has yet found.

There is information that needs to be written in a different way to be found. People want information for whatever they do. They are willing to pay for information if they think it will help them make more than the cost of the information itself.

Americans and non-Americans around the world want information. They want it in any shape or form. On the internet....in a book...an e-book or audio book...CD.....DVD, a movie....in reports or articles.... at a seminar or online webinar....a workshop or a boot camp. It doesn't matter where the information is to be had or in what form----someone will want to buy it.

The benefit of selling information is that the "product" is in near limitless supply. It's constantly being generated. You have a world of information at your fingertips. All you must do is deciding how to organize it, produce, and market it.

Study the following list of infopreneur subjects. Which subjects and services might hold the most interest for many Americans?

- Success and Maturation
- Entrepreneurship
- Headaches
- Advertising
- Time Management

- Marketing
- Sales Training
- Computer Services
- Stress
- Financial Analysis
- Fitness
- Weight Loss
- Cooking
- Internet

What about specializing in services that are offered only to other infopreneurs?

- Internet Webmaster
- Mailing List Broker
- Electronic Services
- Info Marketing Coach
- Speech Coach
- Video Reproduction
- Library Agent
- Audio Producer
- Infomercial Producer
- Public Relations

The key to a thriving infopreneur business is building a large database and creating a lifelong relationship with your customers and/or clients. For example, an author of books on financial information could market his "product" through bookstores like Barnes & Noble, Internet stores like Amazon.com, and through his own Website, too.

The author could promote via carefully targeted E-mails. He might also market his book in audio form. Finally, he might offer seminars and workshops that expand on the information in his books. Your customers will pay a fortune for information that they need today.

Do research on companies that will be your main competitors; find out about their prices, marketing, target market, and anything else that would give you a leg up. Now, can you sell similar information at a lower cost or add more services for the same price?

How will you find your customers? You might advertise on the Internet, TV, or radio, mail letters, send post cards, give seminars, or attend business expos. Select a topic of information that you have a passion for, research it, find out who will buy it, set up your database, package your product, and start marketing it.

Have fun!

Infopreneur Business Ideas To Sell:

Seminar Sales	Personal Consultant
Public Speaker	Professor/Teacher/Trainer
Movies	Calendar Creator
Freelance Writer	Newsletters
E-Books	Internet Expert
Audio-CDs	Reports
Manuals	Home Study
Videos	Posters
Journals	Magazines
Teleconferencing	Radio
Chat Rooms	Telecommunications

Publishing	TV Producer
Books-Author	CD Rom Sales

The final new type of business that you can run from your home and in addition to your other businesses is Internet Marketing.

Internet Marketing Business:

Did you realize that it is possible to make a six or even a seven figure income marketing products on the Internet? In fact, some people make that much money in one month, or even in one week!

How many business opportunities can make money for you while you sleep? How much money could you make if you made 10 cents from each person who uses the Internet? What if you made $500 from one-tenth of 1% of all Internet users? The Internet is an awesome tool. It is like having the whole world in your home office.

There are many different business opportunities and successful strategies to help you make money on the Internet. To understand the basics of Internet marketing, you must first realize that simply creating a Webpage is not enough.

Your Webpage may look very professional, be decorated with beautiful colors and fancy pop-up menus and do nothing to create an Internet-based profit. You must design your Website to sell, and that means starting with a concrete idea of how your product or service will do in the market.

Imagine yourself visiting the Website for the first time, with an interest in purchasing the products listed. What would you need to see? What site design or product descriptions would make you want to spend your hard-earned money? If you search the Internet, it won't take long to find hundreds of confusing Websites. It may be difficult to buy items or may hopelessly confusing or even be impossible to navigate.

If you are interested in creating a successful Internet business, you must either build or have built a marketing website. This means the equivalent of a ready-made business and marketing plan to help sell your products.

Once you have an Internet business marketing plan for your online business, you can focus on giving your Webpage the right colors, fonts, graphics, designs, pop-ups, ordering forms, sales letters, and product descriptions. With your professional Website up and running, how will you drive traffic and potential customers to it?

You're Website:

How do you get people to your site? There are many ways to attract visitors and get them on your Website. Let's discuss some of them. The first way is by marketing your Website address. You should put your Website address on everything you print to help market your business.

For instance, put it on your business cards, stationery, envelopes, bumper stickers, even every E-mail message you send. You can also put your Web address on greeting cards, wedding gifts, on your voice mail message . . . everything.

The second way is through the use of search engines. Remember, it is easier to sell products to customers if they find you themselves by going to your Website or if they E-mail you for additional information on a particular product or service. Why? Simply because they are looking for the type of product or service you are marketing.

They have "chosen" you and that's always good! You will need online search engine companies to send traffic to your site. A typical search could generate thousands, if not millions, of results. There is a wise old saying about ecommerce: "If you don't exist with Google....you don't exist."

Therefore, your goal should be to appear at or near the top of that long, long, list of similar websites. There are at least three ways to help you find the right search engine:

1. *Go to every major search engine and submit your webpage and pray that they will back you.*

2. *Hire a company that will do the work for you by submitting your Webpage to every search engine in the known Internet universe.*

3. *Find a company you can afford that has produced satisfactory to average results. You can also find companies that are willing to charge you on a "per click" basis, or the number of times people visit your site.*

You have absolute control over what kind of hits (keywords, etc.) you receive and how much you will spend each week or each month.

The third way of getting prospects to your Website is by putting an advertisement in an E-zine. Your ad will be read by a large audience who may already be interested in your particular product. It's similar to advertising in a national printed magazine. You can also buy or rent E-mail mailing lists. You will want to rent E-mail mailing lists where the people on the list have already "opted in" and agreed to receive ads from online businesses.

There are lists of E-mail address holders from all over the country or from your specific region. Use these lists to mail direct marketing packages offering them a special report or gift if they are willing send their E-mail address to your Website. Your goal is to build an E-mail database that is so extensive that each time you send out a mass offer you increase your odds of generating sales.

When you have a large E-mail database, the right search engines with your Website listed, and the E-zine ads that work for your products, you will have created the opportunity to reach your internet business goals.

Another way to make money on the Internet, even if you have no products or services, is through affiliate programs. You set up an affiliate program with one or more companies, and each company pays you a commission for each product that is sold through your Website or website link.

You can have as many affiliate programs as you want to. The other part of making revenue through affiliate programs is doing follow-up E-mail marketing. You send e-mails to all of the people who bought the affiliate's product.

Your fortune can be made if you follow prospects, sell existing products, create Internet ads, and even create new products in the future. When you are assembling your Master Mind group, you should add a reputable technology or Internet coordinator to your team.

Internet Marketing Checklist:

_____ Your Unique Selling Proposition (USP).

_____ Catalog.

_____ Automate.

_____ Credit Card and Checks Acceptance.

_____ International Orders.

_____ What Do You Want to Market/Sell?

_____ What Are You an Expert At?

_____ Who Is Your Competition?

_____ Write a Business Plan.

_____ Create a Logo and/or Brand Name.

_____ Determine Your Target Market.

_____ Domain Name(s).

_____ Web Hosting.

_____ Designing Your Website.

_____ Your Sales Letter or Copy.

_____ Your "Shopping Cart."

_____ Delivering Your Products.

_____ Sales and Guarantees to Customers.

_____ Fraud Protection.

_____ Charge Backs, Yes.

_____ Newsletter—Free/Charge.

_____ E-mail Addresses Collection.

_____ Storing E-mail Addresses.

_____ Buying E-mail Lists.

_____ Search Engines.

_____ Directories.

_____ Classified Ads.

_____ E-mail Marketing.

_____ No Spam.

_____ Automating Your E-mails.

_____ Auto Responses.

_____ Testing and Tracking Your Strategies.

You should be ready now to start the process of finding your niche, your business, or what you like to do. You can set up your own lifestyle with the right business. You can set your hours in your business.

Don't ever let a negative person talk you out of doing something you feel good about. A business is a great opportunity, and doing a lot of work doesn't mean it is not enjoyable.

Finally there is a mini-business plan for you write up for whatever business you may like to do. The exercise is to write everything that you know on the business, research and then go over the business plan again.

You should continue to go over your business plan until everything that you find is already listed.

The final plan should be written in a way that, if you opened the business on the first day and you had an accident and you went into a coma, your employees or spouse could run the business from your business plan, step by step.

That's how you need to have it laid out.

Mini-Business Plan:

1. **Business Summary:** *Your mission statement, objectives, and keys to success for the business.*

2. **Company Summary:** *What type of business entity (sole proprietorship, corporation, etc.), the history of business, any sales and profit history, and where business is located. Services and Products: Describe your current products or services, future products and services, costs, sales price, literature, why your products and services are needed, and why customers will buy from you.*

3. **Your Schedule:** *Describe your weekly routine and how you will make sales and profit. What will you do from 8-5 pm or from 6-10 pm each day?*

4. **Marketing Plan and Analysis:** *What market segments will you be marketing to? What are the needs of this market? How big is your market? What are future trends in your market? What is the future growth of your market segments? How will you distribute your products and services to this market? Who is your competition?*

5. **Website Plan:** *What will be your Website marketing plan? Will you offer product and service information, ordering from Website, E-mail sign-up, and/or sales letters?*

6. **Sales and Promotional Strategy:** *You should include all the projected costs and expenses for marketing your products and services. What types of advertising— newspaper, radio, brochures, TV, sales letters, postcards, Internet marketing costs, and/or joint venture marketing or affiliate programs? Project your sales, cost of goods sold, gross profit, expenses, salaries, and taxes for three to five years. You will probably have to do these projections several times. That's okay, the more you do, the better your forecast for a successful business.*

7. **Business Management and Personnel:** *Draw up an organizational chart showing each position in your business. Then describe what each position will do. What will be compensation for each employee—salary or commissions, or both? Will any outside investors be involved with investment of money or time?*

8. **Cash Flow and Balance Sheet Statements:** *Cash flow and balance sheet statements are better forecasting tools than just a projected sales forecast. You will find out very quickly if you will have any cash or assets to carry on if your forecast is wrong. A cash flow pro-forma includes cash received for sales, sales tax received, new loans received, expenses from all categories, accounts payable, loan re-payments anything that will show cash coming in or going out of your business. The balance sheet statement shows your business assets and liabilities and net worth on a month-to-month basis.*

Writing all these things down will give you a track to run on. Plan your work---work your plan!

CHAPTER TWELVE

My Own Blueprint Monitoring

The art of monitoring is more powerful that it might seem. You may think of monitoring as unimportant since it's looking over what you already know. If you think like that, then you might not take monitoring very seriously.

You probably know by now that many things in your life you have learned well were because of practice, and doing the same thing over and over again.

A professional pitcher pitches basically the same way every time. What's hard about that? After all, he's a professional ball player that gets paid to throw a ball. Why does a professional have to practice, if he is already a professional?

Does a professional golfer practice all the time? Most professional golfers have been playing and practicing since they were in their early teens, some at age 6-8. Why does a golfer that finally becomes a professional have to practice?

Take the average professional tournament of four rounds of golf. That's a total of 72 holes times an average of four 'swings' per hole and equals a total of 288 swings per tournament. Can a golfer miss a perfect swing on just 5% of those shots? That equals about 15 shots, which is about four bad shots per round.

Those four swings could have resulted in the minimum amount of strokes, which are called bogeys. A bogey is one over a par and a par is even with the course. That would mean that this professional golfer that had four swings out of 72 was a little off perfect, scoring a 76, four over par. If he does this on the second round, this golfer might not make the cut and consequently be out of the tournament. Just four swings out of 72. That's all it might take to keep a pro golfer out of a tournament.

How does an average American compare with building wealth and net worth? By the time you get to your first 'Monitoring' session, you are still in Little League. It can get even worse, because you might have a fixed 'ego mindset', and think that you are in the major league. Watch out! A bankruptcy is in your future, or at least no more money.

This is why it's so important to monitor everything! You will always learn something new. Then, put that new knowledge into your mindset with everything else you have stored there. It will meld and mesh with the previous learning session to give you the clarity and wisdom needed to make the right decisions.

If you had not gone through the monitoring session, you would have missed 'something' this year, and delayed your progress until you finally learned what you needed to learn.

What is the best way of Monitoring? There are several ways, actually, but one way to stay on top of everything is to meet with some or all your advisor team at least quarterly. If you let your 'ego' go and make decisions without them, you're headed for problems. The thing about this is that you will make some correct decisions and some wrong ones. It may take a few years or months for the full impact of your wrong decisions to come back on you and bite you on your assets.

Before you start this process, you completed a business plan. You have projected the sales, expenses, and profits or losses for the next five years. When you meet with your advisors and go over the projection numbers, you will find out where you stand. This is where the little changes and adjustments start to take place. For example, why aren't you hitting your numbers?

In business, nothing is what it seems. Many times you may feel that you have your business system working the right way; then something new and unexpected happens. This is common, but upsetting because you have not experienced it before. Take a deep breath and correct it. One day it will auto correct.

Now you are on your way to creating your net worth and wealth. You want to own assets in all four of the investment opportunities in America. So now you will draw up some worksheets, 20 worksheets to be exact, for your balance sheet and 20 for your income statement.

On each of the balance sheets, you will put a number from one to twenty and the calendar year starting with your first year. Do the same for the income statement. From these worksheets you will transfer to your business plan each year.

On each of the balance sheets, you will write the four major investment assets:

- Real Estate
- Tax-Plans
- Stock Market
- Business Equity

As you build on each you can have sub-asset accounts for each. Then, you will start with number 20, which is 20 years from your first year, and write down what amount of dollar value you want to have in each asset category. Take your time and put in the numbers. Once you have the 20 year balance sheet, the rest of the 19 years will be easy.

Now, you will put the numbers for your asset categories in the number 19th balance sheet. I hope it will be a lesser number than year 20. Then you proceed to do the next 18 balance sheets the same way. You will probably have to do this several times until it comes out, but this is the greatest 'growth mindset' training for your brain computer in the world. And you are doing it

When you completed the balance sheets, you will do the same to the income statements. The income statements are a little different. You will do the opposite on these twenty statements, marked 1-20. You have to put down all of your income sources and expenses for your first year.

The first year should only show income from salaries or work related income, and zero on your assets. Then you will do the same for years 2-20, and don't forget 'cost of living' raises and bonuses.

When you are finished, make sure that your 1st year sheets match your business plan numbers, too. Make adjustments where necessary. This is not easy. But then again, if only 5-10% of all Americans have a net worth of $500k or more, at least now you know why.

Usually, when things are hard to implement, it's only because you have not experienced it before. It takes time to make it part of your life, like sleeping, eating, bathing, dressing, driving to work, the routine at work, and everything else you do every day.

You will get there!

Now you know what you should do at your monitoring sessions with your advisors. However, go over the twelve parts of your Financial Blueprint at least once a week.

My Own Financial Blueprint:

Money Mindset: This is the hardest one to learn, because it is about change, which is the hardest thing for anyone to do. The best advice for changing your 'fixed mindset' to a 'growth mindset' is to read a minimum of 20 minutes every night before you go to bed. You can read more than that, of course, but read for at least 20 minutes.

It's like filling a big swimming pool with a slow running water hose. The pool will fill up, but it will take hours. It will take a while to change your mindset as you will need to fill it with 'computer files' that were not in there. It can take months or years, and everyone wants to get there fast. If you think that it will take a few years, always remember this: whether you train your mindset or not, those years will pass anyway.

Planning Model: You have to remember the 'P' words, 'planning' and 'procrastinating'. If you are not planning, then you are procrastinating. Planning is key to seeing the future. To see where you are going; to see the mistakes before you make them. You need to have that bird's eye view of what lies below.

Income System: You have to create a structured system of income & expenses, the same way a business does. If you can learn to set aside a percent of all your outflow, expenses or savings, the quicker you will master it, and the quicker you will save more money

Net Worth Model: You need a clear picture of your future net worth, which is hard when you don't have a picture of your current net worth. Write out your net worth, create a picture of your net worth, you have to see it, and touch it create it.

Capital Management: In its simplest terms, you have to manage your present income and expenses before you can make more income. You have to find a way to save, pay off your debt, pay current bills, and manage all of it.

Master Mind Team: There is a quote from Andrew Carnegie, who was one of the first millionaires in America. He gave away almost all of his wealth, valued in today's dollars at over $75 billion dollars. Carnegie said: 'I wish to have as my epitaph: 'Here lies a man who was wise enough to bring into his service men who knew more than he.' Nuff said.

Asset Protection Model: As you build your net worth and assets, you have to protect them from all the 'demons' that want to get your money for nothing. Follow your advisory team's advice and implement each type of asset protection that you can.

The Market: The first investment opportunity, even though you probably have some of your money in the market. The 'Market' is the 'stock market' and the rest of the financial markets. The 'Market' has a lot of everything to invest in. The Market is America.

Tax-Plans: Leverage all you can with Tax-Plans, and try to make IRS your partner more than your enemy. Tax-Deferred, Tax-Free, Taxable, Capital-Gains Taxation, Tax Credits, go over each one and have a diversified Tax-Portfolio.

Real Estate: You can invest in a home, and then invest in more homes, and take advantage of the tax-free exemption on each home that you sell. Invest in rental properties for long term income & appreciation, 'flip a few houses if you are willing to do some hard work, invest in a couple of REITS for commercial properties and diversification of all your real estate net worth.

Business Equity: Today in America you can set up a business anywhere, in your home, away from home, on the Internet, and any kind of business. Find what you like to do, but make sure it can make you profits. And it's not unthinkable to put down that your little business will go Public one day in the future. Just build a business.

Blueprint Monitoring: We are back where we started, and you should keep coming back again and again to review and review.. check and double check.....get advice from your advisory team. Don't ever stop practicing; it keeps you financially fit for life.

Monthly Checklist

_____ Mindset Books
_____ Business Books
_____ Net Worth Chart
_____ Balance Sheets-20
_____ Income Sheet-20
_____ Debt Chart
_____ Tax Brackets
_____ Planning Goals Chart
_____ Calendar
_____ Team Advisors
_____ Home Goals Chart
_____ Income Plan
_____ Business Structure
_____ Infopreneur Model
_____ Internet Model
_____ Business Plan
_____ Action Plan

As you go through the process of building wealth and creating your own 'Blueprint', always remember that if you see yourself doing the same things that you use to do, you are probably back to your fixed mindset. That's okay, changing takes time. Just take some action and do something different.

Index

About the Author

Ruben Ruiz, MSFS, CLU, ChFC, RFC
Author, Financial Advisor & CEO,
The Ruiz Financial Group, LLC

Ruben Ruiz is President and CEO of Money Concepts Financial Planning Centres in San Marcos and San Antonio Texas and The Ruiz Financial Group, LLC. Ruben's firms have a long tradition of helping clients build, manage, and protect their wealth through financial planning and investment advisory services, with an emphasis on retirement worth individuals, baby-boomers, and business owners.

A dedicated financial professional, Ruben speaks with enthusiasm: "My mission is to provide my clients with the finest financial planning and advisory services available in the United States today, in order to help them maintain their family values and achieve their family goals."

Ruben earned his Master of Science in Financial Services (MSFS) degree from the Richard D. Irwin Graduate School of The American College, Bryn Mawr,Pennsylvania.

Ruben holds a Bachelor of Business Administration (BBA) degree from Southwest Texas State University(Texas State University) and has earned the professional designations of Chartered Life Underwriter (CLU) and Chartered Financial Consultant (ChFC).

In recognition of his professionalism, he has received several awards from Money Concepts International,including the Eagles Club, Century Club, Professionals Club. and the coveted Financial Planner of the YearBronze Award. and the Registered Financial Consultant(RFC) in 2000.

Ruben is a member of the Financial Planning Association (FPA) of San Antonio and South Texas, and has served in various positions for the organization, including Chairman of the Board for 1999-2000.

Ruben also served on the International Association of Registered Financial Consultants (IARFC) board of directors for several terms.

He conducts seminars on financial topics and has published articles in local newspapers, as well as a column for the San Marcos Daily Record. He is the author of several financial planning books and articles.

He is resident of Central Texas with his wife, Amanda, and their two children, he enjoys golfing, jogging, racquetball and fitness workouts.

Ruben Ruiz MSFS, CLU, ChFC, RFC
1920 A Corporate Drive, Suite 106,
San Marcos, Texas 78666
Office #: 512-396-2487 / Fax #: 208-279-1073

www.moneyconcepts.com/rruiz

www.myownfinancialblueprint.com

All Securities through Money Concepts Capital Corp.
Member of FINRA/SIPC Registered Investment Advisor with the SEC